The Indigenous Church And The Missionary

Melvin L. Hodges

A Sequel to
The Indigenous Church

William Carey Library

533 HERMOSA STREET • SOUTH PASADENA, CALIF. 91030

In accord with some of the most recent thinking in the academic press, the William Carey Library is pleased to present this scholarly book which has been prepared from an author-edited camera-ready manuscript.

Library of Congress Cataloging in Publication Data

Hodges, Melvin L
    The indigenous church and the missionary.

    Bibliography: p.
    1. Missions. 2. Indigenous church administration.
I. Title.
BV2082.I5H6   266   77-14519
ISBN 0-87808-151-8

Published by the William Carey Library
533 Hermosa Street
South Pasadena, Calif. 91030

PRINTED IN THE UNITED STATES OF AMERICA

Contents

iii

Foreword

Dear Reader:

Melvin Hodges will slip up on you, so do be careful as you read this book. The ideas that he puts on paper are so common sense, down to earth, obviously related to field experience and just as obviously biblically based that you may make the mistake of classifying his book as saying things that are obvious, commonly known, and universally practiced. He has a way of saying things that so much need to be said that you may read his book the first time, like I did his chapters in *Church Growth and Christian Mission,* with the startled question: "So what else is new?"

My experience was to back off, read it again and find that what he said was not necessarily new, but it was dead center of good mission practice and good biblical practice, and it was important because it was so practical and so biblical.

I have used his book, *The Indigenous Church*, for about fifteen years as a required text for nearly every class. There is just one reason for doing it: It makes so much sense that everyone needs to think through these matters of genuine missionary interest. This book takes another turn at discussing current developments as they affect the service of the missionary. Some of the things in the book will make some missionaries uncomfortable. It seems likely that every bit of discomfort felt by a missionary can result in wider usefulness for the missionary and for the nationals with whom he works. Let me commend both the book and the discomfort in the interest of getting on with earth's most important task.

Cal Guy
Professor of Missions
Southwestern Baptist
    Theological Seminary
Fort Worth, Texas

Preface

The author's book, *The Indigenous Church*, was
first published in 1953. It was originally
written for the purpose of offering assistance
to the author's co-workers on the mission field,
particularly those connected with his own
mission. The reception that this book enjoyed
was far greater than anticipated, and a compan-
ion book, *Build My Church*, was produced which
was intended to help national church leaders.
This latter book also had wide acceptance
around the world, and has been translated into
more than a dozen languages.

The Indigenous Church was republished by
Moody Press under the title *On the Mission Field:
The Indigenous Church*, and at a still later date
after some revision, it was given a new title,
Growing Young Churches.

More than twenty years have passed since *The
Indigenous Church* was first published. Missionary co-laborers have suggested that now since

indigenous churches are functioning in most of
the countries in which we labor, that something
should be written to missionaries in their present situation. Thank God that the national
church has developed, with its own officers and
organizational structure. Of necessity, the
role of the missionary has changed as the
national church has come into its own.

To give some assistance to those who are
already in missionary work and to those missionary candidates who are going to the field for
the first time, this little volume, *The
Indigenous Church and the Missionary*, is
offered. In this volume the author attempts to
deal with the problems that the new situation
has produced. However, the scope of the book is
not limited to the solving of problems, but
attempts to show the opportunities for ministry
that exist in working in partnership with the
national church and gives some guidelines as to
how this task may be approached.

It is the author's hope that the present
effort will prove a blessing to those engaged in
missionary labors.

1

The Church's Mission
to Today's World

The term *missions* and *missionary* are likely to
bring widely differing mental images to different persons. Some will envision immediately a
man in a pith helmet about to be devoured by
cannibals. Some may see the same type of individual endeavoring to teach a group of naked
children to read. Others will picture an
austere spinster completely absorbed in civil-
izing and clothing primitive tribes. Still
others see the missionary as a "do-gooder"
engaged in philanthropic efforts of educational
or medical institutions, striving to bring
relief and betterment to underprivileged
peoples. And then, there are those who view
the missionary as an anthropological nuisance
who unnecessarily introduces changes into the
cultural life of the noble and contented
savage.

All such concepts, while perhaps having their
roots in some real-life situations, nevertheless
fail to include the one basic and essential

element of missions. The missionary is above everything else a proclaimer of the good news of the Kingdom of God.

In the first century of the Christian church, the Christian mission was not identifiable in terms of a wealthy nation taking material benefits to an underdeveloped people. Probably the people of Macedonia and Asia Minor were not underprivileged economically or culturally in relation to the sending churches of Antioch or Jerusalem. The mission of the apostles was to share the riches of the gospel of Jesus Christ with those who did not have this knowledge. Today, the cultural and economical facets of missions usually loom larger in the minds of the general public than does the spiritual task of the messenger of Jesus Christ. This confusion in the minds of the people, and often in the minds of missionaries themselves, has often dulled the sharp cutting edge of Christian missions.

We could well wish that the situation were different, and that Christian missions could be defined simply as taking the gospel of Jesus Christ to people that did not have this knowledge, but like it or not, the mission of the evangelical church today is judged in the light of political and economic factors rather than evaluated solely on the basis of the message that the missionary brings. Nevertheless, we reaffirm that in a Biblical sense, mission is not to be confused with cultural or economic factors, but is rather the activity of those who know Jesus Christ in sharing this knowledge with those who do not know Him.

The situation of the underdeveloped countries, especially since World War II, has radically changed. Radio, roads, and the airplane have all contributed to a communication explosion that has

brought these areas closer to the rest of the
world. Education is of highest priority. The
development of national resources, the introduction of manufacturing and increased traffic in
commerce, have all had their profound effect.

In the short span of the writer's own missionary experience he has witnessed the effect of
industrialization of far-removed places and
peoples: a road opening up a new section of a
country, so that in two hours by car, one can
travel the distance that formerly required two
days by horse; a transistor radio on the back-
pack of a Bolivian Highland Indian, providing
music and bringing him into contact with the
larger world, as he himself climbs laboriously
the steep Andean road; crowds of people, young
and old, thronging the streets of a large city
at 10:00 p.m. as night schools finish another
day of classes in adult education--all these are
pungent indications of the changes that are taking place in underdeveloped countries.

Probably one of the greatest single factors
is the emerging of former colonies as sovereign
nations. Among these people, national pride
runs high. These nations are no longer willing
to meekly follow the leadership of the politi-
cally and economically more advanced nations.
They want to occupy in their own right their
place as a nation under the sun. Even in Latin
America, where colonial domination has generally
not been practiced since these nations overthrew
the yoke of Spain and Portugal, the thrust for
national identity is a powerful force. The
United States is castigated for its "economic
colonialism," and nationalism often finds
expression in anti-Yankee speeches and slogans.

CHANGES AFFECT MISSIONARY ACTIVITY

All this could not but affect the position of the missionary from economically developed countries as he seeks to carry on his spiritual ministry. In those countries that were previously colonies of powerful nations, the missionary, because of his own nationality and race, was automatically identified with colonial rule. Often, if he had any difficulties with the local government, he could depend upon the help and backing from the colonial authorities. In Latin America, it was commonly the case that the U.S. citizen, including the missionary, was given preferential treatment. He was often served first in the store and in public office before others who had arrived before him. He was representative of the great and powerful country to the north; he was considered to be better educated, to have more "know how" and to be in many ways superior to the local population. All this has changed rapidly since World War II. Quite often the North American finds that he is the last one to go through immigrations and customs as he enters a country. His nationality, far from making him popular and respected by the local populous, may often prove to be a hindrance to him in establishing good relations.

THE MISSIONARY AND THE NATIONAL CHURCH

There is another element of change that particularly affects the missionary, and this is the development of the overseas church. When the pioneer missionaries went out, they found themselves alone and without a Christian community. Their principal work was that of evangelism and hopefully the establishing of a church. The missionary, as pioneer, was the "father" of the work. He was respected, and often his leadership and decisions were followed without question. In the course of time, by the grace of God, a national church developed. The work grew from three to five or ten churches and finally some kind of a council or conference, was formed. In the beginning, usually the missionary filled a prominent place in the infant church organization.

As the church spread and the national organization became stronger, national ministers began to fill the executive positions and the missionary was no longer the chief executive of the church. In the meantime, other missionaries reached the field to pioneer new areas, or teach in Bible institutes and otherwise help to develop the national church. These were not the original pioneers, and did not enjoy the same prestige that the pioneers did. Further, in some cases, the national pastors often actually had more preaching and administrative experience than did the new missionary. So, today the younger missionary must find his role in the work on a different basis than did the pioneer. Probably 90 percent of missionaries going to the foreign field today find their place alongside of comparatively mature national workers and contribute to an already established church.

It is in this changed world that today's missionary must fulfill God's call. He must understand the role which he is to play in the great drama of church development. If he fails to adjust to these new conditions, he will become frustrated and defeated. If he can learn to accept the new situations and work with them, he has before him a door of unparalled opportunity and response.

THE MISSIONARY TASK TODAY

Faced with these circumstances, many questions arise. What is the true role of today's missionary? What is the missionary task? On what basis should rich America share its financial resources with the undeveloped church overseas?

It is apparent that it becomes a missionary's responsibility to separate the passing from the permanent. He must distinguish between the changing and the changeless. He is called upon to adapt his methods to the requirements of changing times, while at the same time, he must never truncate his message by surrendering eternal truths or principles for the sake of expediency.

The Great Commission rests upon the authority of our living Lord and upon His command to preach the gospel to every creature, and will retain its imperative as long as there are lost men without the knowledge of Christ. The role of the missionary is primarily that of evangelist, church planter, and church developer. He may on occasion find it necessary to fill administrative posts related to the maintenance of the established churches. He may find that circumstances require him to engage temporarily in secular education or do translation work. All of these things he may do as necessity dictates, but he ought not lose sight of the fact that his essential calling--his reason for being a missionary--is evangelism, church planting and development.

The church that the missionary plants on the mission field ought to be of the same spiritual quality as that of the true Church anywhere and in all ages. The Church overseas should share the vitality of the New Testament Church. This signifies that it must accept the responsibility of being a church. This responsibility includes the developing of its own spiritual resources for propagating the gospel to its own people.

It means finding the financial and material
resources necessary for maintaining and expanding the work. It requires that the church overseas develop to become responsible for its own
decisions under the leadership of the Holy
Spirit and in accordance with the Word of God.
These factors are innate in a truly New Testament church. The missionary's contribution
is primarily that of founding and contributing
to the development of this kind of church.

2

New Testament Missions are Church-Oriented Missions

The Church today in general suffers from a weak theology of mission. Mission, in turn, suffers from a weak theology of the Church. Actually, church and mission are two halves of a whole. Mission is the Church in action. The Church in turn is the product of biblical missions. We only deceive ourselves and abort God's purpose when we think of the Church in something other than in New Testament terms, and of the Christian mission as something other than the New Testament mandate.

Biblically, we must consider at least two main aspects of the Church, and there is the suggestion of a third. There is the Church mystical and universal, made up of all true believers in the Lord Jesus Christ, regardless of their race or church affiliation. Then, there are local churches in different cities and communities with their elders, deacons, and members. There is also a suggestion of churches as national or regional units which represent the community of local churches in a given region, such as "the churches of Judea" and the "churches of Asia". In this concept the many local churches in different localities become "the church" of the nation or region (I Cor. 16:9; 2 Cor. 8:1; I Thess. 2:14).

Geography, language, and political barriers cause the churches to fall into different groups. The churches brought into existence upon an island would have a different relationship to each other in the same locality than they would to churches in some distant land who might be totally unknown to them. Denominational churches, of course, were unknown in the New Testament.

THE CHURCH IS OF INTRINSIC VALUE TO GOD

The New Testament shows that God has a special plan and purpose for the Church, both because of what it is to Him, and because of its mission to the world. In that first church council at Jerusalem, James declared that God did visit the Gentiles "to take out of them a people for His name (Acts 15:14). This people became an "elect race, a royal priesthood, and a holy nation; a people for God's own possession" (I Pet. 2:9, ARV). The apostle Paul declared that this Church is to become the bride of Christ (Eph. 5:23-32; see also Rev. 19:7-9). The Church then has a special relationship to God and to the Lord Jesus Christ. Jesus "loved it and gave Himself for it" (Eph. 5:25). This tells of the love of God for the Church for its own sake, both in time and eternity.

THE CHURCH IS GOD'S
INSTRUMENT FOR EVANGELISM

At the same time, the Church is not only a "pearl of great price", for which the Redeemer gave His all, but the Church, while in the world, is God's instrument for the fulfilling of His eternal purpose in the world. Again, Peter reminds us of our mission to the world, "that ye should show forth the praises of Him that has called us out of darkness into His marvelous light" (I Pet. 2:9).

It was to the Church "in embryo" that Jesus said, "Go ye, therefore, and teach all nations, baptizing them in the name of the Father, and of the Son, and of the Holy Ghost; teaching them to observe all things, whatsoever I have commanded you; and lo, I am with you alway, even unto the end of the world" (Matt. 28:19-20). Luke records Christ's words, "But ye shall receive power after that the Holy Ghost has come upon you; and ye shall be witnesses unto me, both in Jerusalem and in all Judea, and in Samaria, and unto the uttermost part of the earth" (Acts 1:8).

So the Church is called to be an instrument for evangelism: to proclaim the good news, nurture converts, and build itself up, both locally and universally, "according to the effectual working in the measure of every part, maketh increase of the body unto the edifying of itself in love" (Eph. 4:16). This then is the Church's responsibility and mission. The fact that we are living in the twentieth century rather than in the first does not alter the commission. Let us therefore explore the mission of the Church to the modern world.

THE NATURE OF THE CHURCH'S MISSION

The Church's mission is a witness to individuals. "Go ye into all the world and preach the gospel to every creature" (Mark 16:5). Every soul has a right to hear the gospel proclaimed by God through Jesus Christ, His Son. As long

as one soul exists that has not had this opportunity, the mission of the Church is unfulfilled.

The Church, however, is more than scattered
individual believers in Jesus Christ. It is a
corporate body (I Cor. 12:13). It is a holy
nation; a special people (I Pet. 2:9-11). It is
an assembly and congregation (Heb. 10:25). The
work of evangelism is not completed until individual believers can be formed into a local
church, which in turn will become God's agent
for spreading the good news of the gospel.

The Christian mission today has often been
weakened and sidetracked from its original purpose. Present-day substitutions for Christian
missions are confusing the issues in many
sections of the Christian church. Social and
political action are being called for instead
of the effort to convert men to faith in Christ.
Some say that the call to individual repentance
is no longer pertinent--that it is rather
society that must repent, since it is the present oppressive society with its inhumanity to
man that produces an ever-increasing harvest of
oppressed individuals who turn to vice and
crime. Converting one individual, they claim,
is of little value as long as the system produces them by the thousands. We are told that
we should not call men to become members of
Christ's Church, since this separates them from
their own people and culture. The argument
here is that the church removes people from
society and builds a wall between them and the
world when the need is for men who will become
incarnate in the world and work for a new social
system. Traditional Christian terms such as
"evangelism", "reconciliation", "repentance",
and "conversion" are used with new meanings to
apply to this concept of social activism.

What is the Christian mission? Is it a benevolent attempt to better social and economic conditions in the world or an attempt to exercise political influence and power?

The term "Christian missions" has fallen into disrepute in some circles as an anachronism. The more popular term today is "Christian mission". *Missions* refers to the now out-dated (they say) concept that the Church must preach the gospel to individuals and establish churches. The Church is in the world as God's mission, and this concept must not be limited to preaching the gospel to the heathen but should be applied to the whole of man and his life. The geographical barriers are blurred between the sending church and the receiving church. The church must think of mission in six continents. At the same time, the distinction between the Church and the world is blurred. The Church is *mission*, we are told. Everything the Church does is *mission*. Sometimes the Church fulfills its mission simply by maintaining the Christian *presence* in a given area or situation.

Certainly there is no quarrel with the idea that everything that Christians are and do should contribute to the growth of the Kingdom of God, and we happily agree that a true Christian presence, the living out of the gospel of Christ, is indispensable. But we do strenuously object to the idea that everything Christians do (honest toil and voting) is *per se* the fulfilling of the Great Commission. The fact that the Christian presence witnesses to the grace of God is not reason to omit or find unnecessary the vigorous *proclamation* of the good news. Whatever term is employed, the biblical interpretation of the Christian mission requires the emphasis of calling men from darkness to light, and the presentation of Jesus Christ as the only Saviour.

Some are saying that the Church should lose itself in society--like a grain of wheat that falls into the ground to die, losing its own identity, and merging with the political forces of revolution in order to bring about a secular "city of God".

James A. Scherer observes,

It is suggested that Black Power, African and Latin American liberation movements might be taken as possible models in interpreting the current quest for salvation . . . . The problem is that contemporary movements add little or nothing to the once-for-all given basis and foundation of the Christian mission in God's reconciling act in Jesus Christ. *The motive and power for mission are not found in the questions and cries of the world,* though from such questions and cries we can get valuable guidance for the direction and carrying out of our mission. Response to human need forms the catalyst, but it is never in itself the motive (1972).

Many examples exist of the misguided enthusiasm of certain church leaders toward a particular political movement, which they believed would benefit the country and the church, only to end up in disappointment. Man cannot foresee the future and he underestimates the forces of corruption at work in the human heart. The answer to the world's needs will never be found in the plans and programs of unregenerate men. Let us remind ourselves of what happened to the Church and to the world in the middle ages when the Church attained political power.

In making these observations, we are not shutting our eyes to the injustices that exist in the world. We are simply stating that the mission of the Church is to preach the gospel of Jesus Christ, which will transform the hearts of men and women and make them new creatures with new desires and a transformed character. We believe this is the only hope for this world. The fact that the Christian faith has not yet brought about a complete transformation of society must be taken in the light of what the Scriptures teach about the course of events, i.e., that evil will increase in the world before the Kingdom comes in power. Also, the fact is that many who call themselves Christians are not necessarily reborn men. They are nominal Christians who have not experienced the transforming power of the Gospel in their lives.

Basically, the Christian believer is "not of this world" (John 17:16). While God is not indifferent to politics, yet He has not chosen the political world as His medium of action in bringing to fruition the redemption of humanity. His chosen instrumentality is the Church. While God has a plan for this world, the Scriptures do not indicate that the Church should join arm in arm with ungodly and atheistic forces to bring about a remedy to cure its ills. Rather, His people will recognize the Lordship of the Redeemer, place themselves in His hands to do His bidding in carrying His gospel to the ends of the earth, and thus be "the light of the world" and "the salt of the earth."

Again Scherer declares, "The Christian mission can include no less than the full Christological witness to salvation and grace in Jesus Christ. The suppression of the witness is unthinkable, for the name and power are inseparable" (Scherer 1972).

True Christianity calls for the intervention of God Himself in the person of Jesus Christ in order to establish righteousness upon the earth. We must not confuse the biblical mission of the Church with the humanistic ideas of natural man.

The Church is to be planted in every land. We have already pointed out that the Church is to be an instrument for evangelism. This means that the Church which is to result from missionary effort must be the Church in the true sense of the word. It must be New Testament in doctrine, experience, and power. It is not enough to establish a branch of a Christian church that depends on the United States or Europe for the supplying of its needs. The Church must be the CHURCH, and the Church that is brought into existence through the proper preaching of the Word, through the power of the Holy Spirit, will have the basic characteristics of the New Testament church. Something is amiss if we bring into existence a church that is weak, dependent, and without initiative.

It goes without saying that the Western world can never send enough missionaries to do the work of evangelism that is required to reach the multiplied millions who are yet without Christ. It is also an accepted fact that Western churches cannot produce enough workers or pastors to take care of the churches that will spring up. This means that the church that is raised up on the foreign field must be endued with the same missionary spirit as was the church that sent the missionary out to evangelize in the first place. Anything less will not meet the requirements to today's world. When the church is planted, it becomes the normal agency through which God will work to continue the task of total evangelism.

The stability and growth of a budding church requires that it be firmly established in the Word of God. Paul attributed the stability of the church in Thessalonica to the fact that the Word had penetrated the lives of the believers (I Thess. 2:13; see also Acts 2:42). The teaching of the Word must be given to all believers, and not just to those who may become leaders, for the entire congregation needs to be well rooted in the truths of the gospel.

One of the most important factors in establishing a church is the development of national leadership. This leadership must be truly called of God and filled with the Spirit, for it is the Holy Spirit with His anointing and spiritual gifts that provides the indispensable preparation for the work of the ministry. Moreover, such men require training for their task. Without question, one of the greatest contributions of missions, outside of evangelism itself, is the developing of national leaders who can guide their people with blessing, wisdom, and power, not only into Christian maturity, but for the continuing of the task of total evangelism.

The church developed on the mission field shares also the missionary responsibility. It is not enough that the church be trained to maintain itself, but it must partake of the apostolic spirit and engage in evangelism to its own people and send out workers to the unevangelized even beyond its borders.

3

The Missionary's Partnership with the Overseas Church

In the first chapter it was pointed out that the status of the missionary has been changed considerably due to the political and economical factors that have been at work these last decades. His relationship with the national church is on a different basis than was that of the pioneer missionary who arrived in the country to establish a church. These factors bring into sharp focus the necessity of the missionary to understand his present role.

HOW PERMANENT IS THE MISSIONARY MINISTRY?

At this point, the question arises as to how permanent is the ministry of a missionary is in a given area. In an earlier book, *The Indigenous Church* (1953), the author made the comparison of the ministry of the missionary to that of a scaffolding on a building. The object, it was stated, is to build the building, which in this case, is the church, and when the church is built, the scaffolding is taken down, as it is

not a part of the permanent structure. In this
we have the example of the apostle Paul who
founded the church in different cities and
countries and then passed on to continue his
ministry in other areas. He did not consider
himself as a permanent part of any local church.
This viewpoint has raised considerable objec-
tions on the part of some missionary leaders and
national ministers. One African national church
leader has stated that the African church wants
missionaries who will put down their roots and
give their lives for the church. They were not
interested in a temporary ministry. It seems
evident that both viewpoints have validity. It
must be understood that two different emphases
are in mind.

In comparing the missionary as scaffolding
and using the familiar term that "the missionary
should work himself out of a job," it should be
remembered that the point of emphasis is that
the missionary should develop national church
leadership rather than consider himself the
permanent leader of the church. Much has tran-
spired since those viewpoints were expressed.
At that time in some cases, missionaries were
pastoring churches that had had missionary
pastors for a whole generation, and there was
still no national leader capable of taking over.
Missionaries were often considered automatically
to be the superintendents of the work. The
statement that the missionary should consider
himself as scaffolding of temporary usefulness
*was intended to emphasize the need of the
missionary to plant a church that would be able
to support itself, govern itself, and propagate
itself.* The New Testament example is strongly
behind this viewpoint. The missionary's task
is to mature the church and raise up the
necessary leaders. Nationals should be pastors,
should fill the national organization's

official posts, and the time should come when
national leaders should also become instructors
and presidents of the Bible institutes. The
church on the foreign field should be complete.
It is an inadequate concept to maintain that any
area of the church's life must *permanently* be
supplied from a foreign country.

However, these concepts were never intended
to convey the idea that the missionary had
nothing left to offer the national church once
a national leadership is developed. Paul
strengthened the churches that he raised up by
repeated visits and by writing letters to them.
While the missionary may no longer be the superintendent of the national organization or pastor
the principal churches, his ministry may still
be required for the extension and maturing of
the church in many different areas.

ALL MISSIONARY MINISTRIES
ARE NOT THE SAME

Actually, all missionary ministries are not
the same. Paul recognized this. To the
Corinthian Church he stated, "I have planted and
Apollos has watered, but God gave the increase"
(I Cor. 3:6). Some missionaries have distinc-
tive pioneer ministries for establishing the
church. Others have a very important and
essential ministry in "watering" the church.
Paul left Titus in Crete for such a missionary
ministry: to "set in order the things which
were wanting" (Titus 1:5). Timothy also evidently had such a "watering" ministry among the
churches. He was left in Ephesus by Paul to
strengthen that church which was troubled by
false doctrines (I Tim. 1:3,4).

Missionaries going out into the foreign field today will often find a national church already in existence. Pioneer missionaries who have planted the church in the beginning and are still on the field will rejoice that their ministry has been fruitful inasmuch as they have brought into existence a church that is able to govern itself and develop ministries that will edify and mature the church. Rather than feeling rejected, they should find this a cause for rejoicing.

As circumstances change, the Holy Spirit will also change the ministry of the missionaries to meet the different needs. Among the overseas churches there is a great need for teaching. Teaching in the Bible institutes or Bible colleges offers missionaries a challenging opportunity where some may well spend the rest of their years contributing to the development of the national leadership. There are also ministries of literature, of radio, correspondence schools, and evangelistic campaigns. Often there are areas in the country where the church has not yet been planted, and the missionary can return to his primary calling of a church planter.

TENSIONS RESULTING FROM CHANGE

As could be expected, this change of roles on the part of a missionary and his relationship to the national church can be tension-producing. Both the missionary and the national church may experience difficulty in finding the proper relationship to each other. The fact that a changed situation has produced tensions is acknowledged by all. As the national church reaches maturity, the missionary is no longer *over* the national church. Some mission boards have gone to the extreme of placing the missionary *under* the national church. In fact, the missionary is sometimes no longer called by

that name. He is called a "fraternal worker".
Even his finances may be handled through the
national church, and he is assigned his task by
the executives of the national organization.

Certainly, we agree that missionaries should
have the spiritual maturity to serve under the
national church if this would be required. The
Bible tells us to submit ourselves one to
another, for all of us to be clothed with
humility. Without question, such arrangements
give ample opportunities for the missionary to
demonstrate Christian character in his humility
and willingness to serve his brethren. Also,
it demonstrates the truth that in Christ there
are no racial distinctions. However, serious
doubts do exist as to whether this procedure is
really productive. Many problems and frustrations arise with this arrangement. It seems in
part to be artificial, imposed on the missionary
rather than growing out of his calling and
ministry.

Two things must be kept in mind in consider-
ing this. In the first place, the missionary is
sent to fulfill a ministry in which church
planting and church maturing have priority.
There is a distinct possibility that the
national leaders may not have the same vision
for the growth of the church, and that instead
of producing greater church growth, making the
missionary's assignment entirely subject to the
national executives, they could actually hinder
it. We have known of cases where, if the
national organization or a superintendent had
had his say, a missionary would have been placed
as an assistant to a national pastor. Other
missionaries have expressed concern that they
might be removed from an evangelistic ministry
and placed as supervisors of day schools. Some
missionaries have found their situation so frustrating that they have left the field.

The missionary's personal call of God is involved in this matter. The Holy Spirit endows men with gifts for certain ministries, and we must not consent to an arrangement whereby the will of God is not permitted to find fruition because of arbitrary decisions.

MISSIONARY AND NATIONAL
CHURCH RELATIONSHIPS

The ideal situation is for the missionaries to enter into a partnership with the national church. Some mission groups have opted for a complete separation between the national church and the mission. Missionaries in this case are not members of the national church, can hold no offices in the national church, but operate a parallel organization, and meet in consultation with the leaders of the national church to offer the church certain services which the church still needs. This procedure is unavoidable where the missionary body is seeking to serve a national church that was established, perhaps by the national Christians themselves, previous to the coming of the missionary. The missionary did not grow up with the church, and now if he is to serve it, it must be by offering services which the national church is not yet capable of performing. This could well take the form of providing literature or of establishing a Bible institute for the training of the national pastors of that group. Even so, the more integrated that he can become in brotherly love and confidence with the national church, the more fruitful his ministry will be.

Personally, I would favor integration of the missionary into the national church where this is possible. It seems to be beneficial for the missionary to be considered as a member of the national church while it is young and struggling toward maturity. For a time, the missionary can serve as a superintendent and show the way. The vision and energy of the missionary sets an example for the church that is just learning to take its first steps. We have seen a national church stagnate because of having leaders who were not yet mature, or experienced enough to lead a national organization.

When a national is placed as leader of the work before he has the experience and has developed his administrative gifts sufficiently, it sometimes happens that he depends on the missionary for guidance. This, of course, is helpful, but unfortunately this dependence often produces dissatisfaction among the pastors. They tend to see the leader as the missionary's man, and may finally reject him as a puppet. In such cases, the missionary is still the actual leader of the work, and it would seem better for him to openly assume this responsibility until nationals are prepared to take it.

The danger, of course, in permitting the missionaries to hold offices in the national church is that they may continue in such posts too long and consider themselves as the rightful leaders of the national church, rather than attempting to develop the leadership of the nationals themselves. However, where there is spiritual vision and understanding of the goals, it should not be difficult for missionaries to recognize the point at which they should not permit their names to be considered any longer for official posts so that the national brethren may occupy these positions.

However the details may be worked out, we believe that a partnership arrangement is ideal. The missionary is neither *over* nor *under* the national church, but working alongside the church as a fellow worker. It is interesting to note that the Division of Foreign Missions of the Assemblies of God has tooled out the following statement to define this relationship.

> The missionary is the servant of the Lord in the implementation of the Great Commission and in every respect is to seek the enhancement of the national church. Missionary field councils or representatives shall through dialogue and mutual agreement seek to work together with the national church in the common cause of winning the lost and further establishing indigenous New Testament churches. It is understood that such cooperation implies neither "absorption into" nor "exclusion from" the national church.
>
> The missionary must be flexible, for his role will change as the national church matures. The actual missionary-national relationship will be determined by the need for cooperation and unity in the mutual God-given responsibility for complete world evangelization. In so doing, the missionary must not abdicate his responsibility to world evangelism and church planting, neither by perpetuating the mission's authority over the national church nor by succumbing to nationalistic interests that would prevent him from fulfilling the Great Commission (*The Missionary Manual of the Assemblies of God*).

OPEN DISCUSSION

The question of a missionary's location and assignment requires open discussion and communication. In the placing of a missionary, the

missionary organization should not have the
total say, nor should the national church be the
the only voice that decides this question.
Three things are involved: first, the purpose
of the missionary body in sending the missionary
to the field; second, the desires of the national executives as they see the needs of the field;
and third, the individual calling of the missionary himself. The missionary cannot do his best
work if he does not feel that he is in the place
where God wants him to serve. Therefore, these
three factors should line up, not by arbitrary
decisions of any one of the three, but by prayer-
ful consultation. Since the Holy Spirit is in
charge of the Church, this is not an impossible
solution. God can guide so that the decision
reached is satisfactory to all concerned.

RECOGNITION OF NATIONAL CHURCH AUTHORITY

In the final analysis, of course, the national church is the official organization in the
country, and the missionary is there by the consent of the foreign government and in a certain
sense he is a guest of the church. If the
matters reach an impasse, it is entirely
possible that the national church would have
final say with the government as to whether a
visa could be granted. In such a case, the
individual missionary will have to seek God to
know how he should proceed if the decision of
the national church is not in harmony with his
own convictions. However, it is our experience
that missionaries who have an anointed ministry,
a godly Christian character, and humility
enough to acknowledge the authority of the
national church and work with it, usually have
no trouble in finding an open door. In fact, in
spite of anti-missionary and anti-American senti-
ment, I have yet to see the national church close
the doors to a missionary with an anointed ministry and a proper attitude toward his brethren.

4

Establishing a Partnership with the National Church

We shall now examine the factors that must be taken into consideration in establishing a viable partnership with the national church. We are at present concerned with the missionary who works in a country where a national church has come into existence either through his own efforts or the efforts of others. All the executive officers of the church are now national brethren. The original pioneer effort of the missionary in getting the church started has been accomplished. The missionary, however, is staying on in the country to "water" the budding church and must enter into a working partnership with the church. He needs to find a place of fulfillment for his ministry where he can make a valuable contribution to the church, and yet avoid tension-producing situations. Vergil Gerber states the situation succinctly in the following phrases: "Churches produced missions. Missions produced churches. Their success produced tensions" (Wagner 1972).

CAUSES FOR TENSIONS

Culturally oriented tensions

Many of the tensions that arise between
missionaries and nationals are culturally
oriented. While some of these things cannot be
helped because of the differences in background,
yet by being aware of their existence, the missionary can help to minimize them.

A frequent complaint against certain missionaries is the fact that they *do not speak the
language well*. We have known of students in
Bible schools to complain that they do not understand what the missionary is trying to teach
them. Perhaps it would not be going too far to
state that many missionaries overestimate their
ability in the language. They sometimes think
that they speak better than they do. This is a
constant challenge and requires continual effort.
The missionary should not discontinue language
study because he is able to carry on a conversation. He should study the language as long as
he ministers to a people. Newspapers in the
vernacular should be read along with books by
native authors. Observe the phrases used by the
best speakers.

Another similar complaint is that the missionary *does not understand the national*. This is
particularly true of the missionary that continually uses conditions in the United States as a
constant frame of reference. Also, the missionary may not be aware that he inadvertently at
times goes against the customs of the people.

North Americans are noted for their frank
approach. They are often in a hurry and want to
get to the point without unnecessary preliminar-
ies. Nationals in many areas prefer the oblique

approach and avoid the direct statement, especially when it has to do with some form of accusation or judgment. They may not be so concerned with saving time as in not offending. An apparent assent may not really mean "yes", and if the missionary assumes that it does, he may find himself facing again the same problem when he thought that the matter had been settled. The missionary must become sensitive to the meaning behind oblique statements, and also he should attempt to moderate his own frankness and learn to convey thoughts and judgments in the same way that the nationals do.

Open discussion is essential to understanding. In this he must be careful not to monopolize conversation in order to get his point across. He should not do all the talking in committee meetings. Rather, he should encourage his fellow members to speak up. He must make room for the extra time required, and not become frustrated with indirect approaches. By doing these things, perchance he may attain a degree of confidence and sharing with his brethren, so that meaningful decisions can be reached to the satisfaction of all concerned.

Many times the North American missionary is thought to be *proud*. Sometimes this impression is communicated simply because the new missionary is not free in the language and rather than to make a mistake, he prefers to remain silent. His lack of communication could be mistaken for pride. It is better to make the effort to converse, even though mistakes are made in the language, than to give the impression of aloofness.

Although the missionary may be misunderstood at times, yet the *feeling of superiority* is something that the American missionary must

constantly guard against. It can be manifested
in so many different ways without the missionary
even being aware of it. The missionary's education is often superior to that of those to whom
he ministers. Then he probably enjoys a better
financial position. This is manifested in his
equipment and standard of living. This superiority may be manifested in the comparisons
which the missionary makes between the customs
of the people where he is working and the
customs of his own homeland. His attitude
toward his possessions is important. The spirit
of *sharing* in God's work will help reduce
tensions.

When a missionary by-passes the authority of
the national church executives, he will certainly
be considered as manifesting superiority. Such
action shows the national that the missionary
considers himself to be above the authority of
the church.

There is sometimes the question as to whether
the missionary *really loves* the people to whom
he is ministering. Again, the missionary is
open to misunderstanding in the area of financial help to the churches and to the pastors.
He may desire wholeheartedly to develop initiative and responsibility in pastors and churches
and thus refrain from making them dependent
upon his financial help. This can very well be
misinterpreted by some as lack of concern and
love. Without sacrificing his ideal, the
missionary must find ways to manifest his love
other than by financial help.

Then there is the question of hospitality.
Some missionaries do not invite nationals into
missionary homes on the basis of friendship.
This again is interpreted as stemming from a
feeling of superiority and of lack of real
friendship for the people.

To counterbalance these things, the missionary must attempt to develop sincere friendships and show interest in the national people. He can demonstrate that there is real love and concern in his heart by the way that he acts. Happily, nationals are usually highly intuitive in most cases and are able to discern a person's real thoughts and intent. It is not necessary for the missionary to make a statement to the effect that he loves them. His true feelings will show through and will win a response.

Of course, the matter is not one-sided. The missionary also may see things in the nationals that he does not approve of or which he may not understand. The missionary should be careful in making general statements. He should avoid categorizing the people as a group. For example: "These people are all liars"; "These people cannot be trusted". There are untrustworthy people in every society, including the missionary's homeland. All people are not alike. Such generalizations reflect a lack of penetration on the part of the speaker in the knowledge of the people and their culture.

However, the missionary may find that some nationals do not measure up to his standards in their responsibility in handling of funds. Some Christian concepts are attained only with Christian maturity. Patience is required. They may seem also to handle the truth loosely. This often must be interpreted in a cultural context. What might be a "lie" to a missionary may not be a lie to a national because both the one speaking and the person hearing understand what is really meant. True, nationals may not keep appointments on time and may be as much as an hour late to important meetings. These concepts are often culturally oriented, and it is the missionary that must make the adjustment. A

Colombian asks, "Why should North Americans require strict punctuality in countries where the people keep their appointments by thinking in terms of hours rather than minutes? Why demand that work be delivered on time when the term *manana* really only gives a certain degree of hope that the work will be eventually finished?" (Marquez, n.d.).

The missionary should avoid categorizing anyone as "stupid". This is a very offensive word and reveals more about the person that uses the term than it does about the person of whom it is spoken.

Some missionaries have developed tensions with the nationals because they have assumed that the nationals are looking for financial advantage and that the missionary or his equipment is just something that the national wants to "use". It will help the missionary to endeavor to see these things from the national's viewpoint. The missionary seems to have so much in comparison to the national. It is difficult for them to be objective. Some nationals, like their North American counterparts, are grasping, and cannot be trusted. Care must be taken not to fall victim to their wiles, for this will mark the missionary as an "easy-touch". However, again we must not generalize and place all in the same category. Some are as sincere and generous as the missionary himself and are fully trustworthy. It is an injustice to look upon *all* with suspicion.

The fact that nationals do not always carry a project to conclusion or seem to lack initiative in these matters may also be annoying to the missionary. The missionary might examine the project under consideration to see if the project has really been accepted as the national's

own. The lack of enthusiasm may stem from the
fact that he never really was convinced of its
necessity.

The lack of sanitation may become a tension-
producing factor in the missionary's relationships with the nationals. Reasonable care must
be taken to protect one's personal health and
that of the family. However, some missionaries
have become so "germ conscious" in their concern
about water, food, and personal contacts, that a
psychological barrier is raised between themselves and the nationals. Reasonable care for
health is advisable, but love should so fill the
heart, that the concern is not primarily for
one's own safety, but rather to find the way of
ministering to need. After all, the missionary
goes to the foreign field, not to save his life,
but to lose it; not to minister to himself, but
to others.

Slowness of individual response and lack of
initiative can also be irritating to the missionary. This problem is usually culturally
oriented, and if the missionary becomes aware of
the reasons, it will help him to be more patient.
For example, sometimes the missionary deals with
people who have been accustomed all their life
to take orders from others. They have worked on
plantations or haciendas. They carry over a
certain passivity into their life in the church.
It will take careful guidance and time for such
an individual to understand that as God's child,
filled with the Spirit, he too can make a contribution to the church. Again, in some cultures,
the individual is not expected to act on his own.
He has always understood that important decisions are made by the family or the clan, and he
does not feel comfortable when he is asked to
make an individual decision without consulting
with others.

In all of this the missionary should remember that he is called of God to minister to this people and that God will help him over the hurdles. There will be problems and difficulties to be ironed out. Hopefully, the missionary will learn to look at things through the national's eyes. While he is in the process of learning these things, he does have recourse to the love of God which the Holy Spirit will shed abroad in his heart. Love is the bond of perfectness and the language of the heart. Tensions will be reduced and causes for difficulty minimized when love is truly manifest in our lives.

Organizationally-Oriented Tensions

The missionary's attitudes may be involved in a tension-producing situation. It could be that he may unconsciously suffer from a feeling of rejection. Possibly he has carried over from a previous period of ministry certain concepts concerning his ministry and his place in the national work, which while valid at one time, no longer obtain in the new situation. The initiative of the nationals in leadership may be interpreted as "anti-missionary", especially if the missionaries are not consulted in the decisions reached. This feeling of rejection may cause the missionary to resent the action and decisions of the national executives and consequently produce tensions in their relationships. Of course, the answer is for the missionary to take a square look at his own motives and at his goals in missionary work.

Along with this a missionary may attach too much importance to executive posts. Having been superintendent or having filled some other important position in the work, he now feels that he must take a secondary role, and that actually his ministry is less important than it was before. It will help us to remember that the missionary's ministry is not primarily one of administrative responsibility and that the larger percent of administration has to do with maintaining the work and keeping the wheels of the organization running smoothly.

The primary ministry of a missionary is that of pioneer and church planter. Therefore, for a missionary to be tied down with executive responsibilities, which perhaps while building the ego, may actually prove to be less fruitful in the area of ministry. Rather than a missionary resenting the fact that he is no longer filling executive posts, he should rejoice that he is now given the opportunity of fulfilling his more basic calling of planting and maturing the church.

Another cause of tensions and frustrations in this area is the fact that nationals are often immature and perhaps not as capable as the missionaries themselves. This is to be expected. We all learn by doing and the national is no exception. It is also true that often the man that is the most desirous of executive posts is the least prepared spiritually for this responsibility. There is no question that some nationals are wrongly motivated in seeking that nationals rather than missionaries occupy executive posts. While some have the proper attitude and believe that the work would progress better under national leadership, others may be inspired by the motivation of personal ambition and this can only produce friction and some measure of failure.

The missionary is called upon to exercise spiritual maturity in these circumstances. His faith in the Holy Spirit's ability to bring the

Church through victoriously needs to be coupled
with patience and tact. Every missionary at
such a time feels the need for divine wisdom and
guidance. Perhaps the national church will make
a mistake and put the wrong man into office. Let
the missionary be slow to judge this, and give
his full cooperation, even if the man elected is
not his own choice. Both the missionary and the
church may learn valuable and necessary lessons
through this experience. Missionaries sometimes
have their own areas of carnality, and these
circumstances are ideal means of showing them
up! Given time the rough areas are likely to
smooth out and understanding and happy relationships become the norm.

THE GOAL OF HARMONIOUS RELATIONSHIPS

In a chapter called "Polarization and Harmony"
which the author contributed to the book *Church/
Missions Tensions Today*, there is outlined
briefly the path that the Assemblies of God
missionaries have ordinarily taken to obtain
a goal of national-missionary equality.

In order to attain this goal, a national
organization has been formed early in the
history of the work in each country, with
a constitution which places the missionary
and the national pastor on the same level
of privilege. Election to official positions is limited only by the ability of
each worker to meet the requirements of
the constitution and to secure the backing
of fellow workers. In several cases,
national organizations have begun with as
few as four or five churches. Quite logically, the missionaries fill posts of
leadership in the beginning, since they
have brought the work into existence, and
the younger workers who are pastoring

prefer that a missionary take this responsibility. In this position, the missionary teaches by example in the same manner
that he has led the way in the development
of other areas of church life. It is
specifically desired that nationals fill
all posts for which they are eligible.
Often in the beginning, certain limitations of the constitution, requiring a
stipulated degree of experience in the
ministry for certain offices, are temporarily suspended to allow new workers to
participate. This helps avoid a mission-
ary-dominated organization. Admittedly,
this procedure is somewhat risky, but we
have not been disappointed in the outcome.

Usually our missionaries, attuned to the
political climate of the country and being
aware of the advantage of national
brethren making their own decisions, seek
to be relieved of their administrative
posts as soon as possible. In a few cases
they have insisted on this even before it
seemed that the national ministers were
actually ready for the change.

Since there are no restrictions on nationals filling executive positions, as soon
as they have obtained sufficient maturity
and experience to command the respect of
their own brethren, there is a minimum of
feeling that the missionary is smothering
national initiative. This greatly miti-
gates against a "power struggle" between
missionaries and nationals. In most cases,
the transition to complete national leadership has been achieved without serious
tensions.

However, since people are still people, some risks are involved. Usually before national leadership is attained with a corresponding partnership participation on the part of the missionaries, a certain oscillation between extreme positions is experienced. The progress has been more or less as follows:

1. The work is originally develops in missionaries prominent in leadership.

2. A national leadership develops in this situation, and usually if relationships between missionaries and national pastors have been wholesome and cordial, the first national superintendent will be someone close to the missionaries who has worked with them.

3. Often if the national superintendent is too much of a follower and depends too much on the missionaries, some dissatisfaction is likely to develop against him on the part of the more aggressive national leaders. They may complain that although the missionary is not superintendent, he is actually running the field through the superintendent who is more or less a puppet.

4. The reaction against the national superintendent in this case may develop to the point that someone with more radical tendencies is placed in the office. At this stage, some of the nationals may be a little overconfident and the missionaries may feel that their ministry in the country is threatened. They may even feel unwanted. This is where maturity,

understanding, and patience on the part of the missionary must be exercised.

5. At this juncture, one of two developments may transpire:

a. The strong nationalistic leader may push his point of view too far, and a reaction against his policies may be the result. Being young and without too much experience, he may push his point of view so far that the more conservative element begins to assert itself again. The leader may find himself without sufficient following, and the post may go to someone else; either a missionary may be returned temporarily to the office, or a more moderate national leader, who can avoid polarizing his position, will be placed in control. This latter creates a position whereby missionaries can work out a partnership relationship with the national church and enjoy fruit and growth for a long period.

b. The nationalistic leader may quickly learn that the work is more difficult than he had anticipated, and modify his extreme position. If he comes to the conclusion that the missionary is not a threat to his position of leadership, a better understanding may be reached and he may come to the missionary for counsel and guidance in difficult questions.

Happily, many of the fields have avoided the problems of extremism, so the transition to complete national leadership has taken place in a tension-free atmosphere. So much depends upon the personalities involved; the greater the maturity and leadership among both nationals and missionaries, the smoother the transition will be (Wagner 1972).

PARTNERSHIP STRUCTURES

Good relationships do not simply happen. They must be prayed about, planned for, and worked at patiently and consistently.

It will help to have some kind of structured relationship. There should be some channel through which the missionaries can approach the national executives, and also through which the national executives can approach the missionaries in regard to problems or plans. Several of the national churches of their own accord have made room on their national executive committee for a missionary representative. He may be there with or without vote, but he is there to monitor the attitudes of the national brethren and take note of the decisions made and convey these to the missionary body. Also he represents the missionary body to the executive brethren for any project or problem that they may desire to present. This has proved very helpful.

Another device which we have found very helpful in ironing out missionary relations with the national executives is to call joint sessions in which all the leaders of the national church in all departments are present along with the entire missionary staff in which they can talk over together the areas of relationships, problems, projects, and plans for the future, giving liberty for everyone to express his opinion. This provides an opportunity to work out tensions that may have developed and to also help the missionary find those areas of ministry where he can best serve the work. Such meetings should be planned at least once a year.

Whatever the structure, it is of utmost importance to have some medium of communication.
Otherwise frustrations and tensions develop on
both sides.

The writer recalls several occasions when he
found it advisable as field secretary to call a
joint meeting of national executives and missionaries. In these cases the national executive
body was made up completely of national leaders,
and missionaries had not a place in the administration of the work. In a couple of instances
a missionary did sit as missionary representative in the national executive committee meetings. However, tensions developed, as missionaries in general felt "out of it". They were
not aware of the thinking of the national
brethren, and in turn, the national brethren
were not well informed of the plans and
activities of the missionaries. This gave room
for suspicions and misunderstandings. We
suggested a united conference in which both
sides could air their complaints and ask
questions. In every case it resulted in clear-
ing the atmosphere and the bettering of relationships. Sometimes there were legitimate
complaints and the causes needed to be corrected.
Other times the matter was cleared up with
explanations of what had actually happened. It
was after observing the results of unity which
such meetings produced that the writer urged
that missionaries and national executives meet
together at least once a year in planning
sessions, in order to keep relationships on the
highest possible level of understanding.

THE MISSIONARY FIELD FELLOWSHIP

Up to this point, we have been more concerned
about the individual missionary and his relationship to the national church. However, the

missionary does not deal with the national
church simply as an individual, but as one of a
group of missionaries that has entered into a
partnership with the national church in carrying
out the Great Commission. There are advantages
in having this relationship structured for the
best possible relationships among the missionaries and to the national church.

One mission approaches the matter of mission-
ary/national relations as follows:

> The major objective of the Missionary
> Field Fellowship shall be the establish-
> ing of an indigenous church. As soon as
> possible, a national organization shall
> be brought into being. After its estab-
> lishment, all matters pertaining to the
> Church should be delegated to this
> national organization. The Field Fellow-
> ship should then concern itself exclu-
> sively with matters relating to the
> personal life of the missionary in con-
> trast to his ministry in and on behalf of
> the national church (*Missionary Manual
> of the Assemblies of God*).

It is to be noted that there are limitations
placed on the Field Fellowship in an effort to
assure that the missionaries do not usurp the
prerogatives of the national organization, nor
vote in the national conventions as a block.
When either of these situations occur they produce tensions and are frustrating to the
national leadership.

However, such restrictions should not be
interpreted to mean that the Field Fellowship is
so separate from the national church that it
cannot so much as discuss the matters that concern it. This would be unrealistic, for

missionaries are on the field to work with the
national church, and it is important that
missionaries discuss the problems and programs
so that they reach an understanding and concen-
sus among themselves.

For example, we have already explained that
the place where a missionary is to be stationed
should be worked out with the national church,
and with the representatives of the mission,
taking into account the missionary's own calling
and sense of divine direction. To give a
recommendation on this point certainly affects
the national church. In fact, the strategic
placing of missionaries with a proper assignment
is one of the greatest contributions the mission
can make toward the development of the national
church.

Other things also come into focus, such as
whether a given project merits a loan of
missions funds. Again, what area of the country
needs development, and what can the mission do
to stimulate the needed growth? These are
questions that affect the national church which
must be discussed by the Field Fellowship. Also,
the missionaries should come to some united
understanding as to how funds will be handled,
and if gifts are to be given to the national
church, how they will be channeled. The restric-
tion mentioned above is intended to insure that
decisions belonging to the national church, such
as issuing credentials to a worker, or placing
a pastor, shall not be usurped by the missionary.

It is important that the Missionary Field
Fellowship operate in a way that will produce
harmony among the missionaries themselves and
understanding and cooperation with the national
church. Great care must be taken, however, to
insure that these deliberations of the

missionary body do not in any way invade the prerogatives of the national church, but simply
form the basis for discussion and interchange
with the national officials or in the national
assembly. The missionary should maintain an
awareness of the influence of his words and
position, and not use these advantages in a way
that will stifle the proper initiative in decision making on the part of the national church
itself.

Of course, it is necessary that both the
missionaries and the national executives
approach the area of relationships with proper
attitudes. The missionary must accept the
national executives in their role and not carry
over relationships based on the past when the
man that is now a national leader was once just
a student in school or a young preacher. Some
missionaries have taken the attitude, "Well, he
may be the national superintendent, but I
remember the little town where he came from and
for me he will always be just 'Little John'."

Missionaries must honor agreements that are
reached in the national church even when they
have not originated with them. If the missionary is a member of the national organization, he
probably will have the same responsibilities,
financial and otherwise, that fall upon the
national workers and these should be honored,
although there may be special cases where some
adjustment would have to be made because of
financial obligations elsewhere.

Also, the missionary should not bypass the
national executive. It is extremely frustrating
to the national officer who is purportedly in
charge of a certain section of the work to have
the missionary disregard him and handle a

problem unilaterally as though there were no superintendent, secretary, or presbyter involved.

Spiritual maturity is the key. There has never been a time in the history of missions when the missionary enterprise needed men of mature spiritual character, with the fruit of the Spirit, more than today. Naturally, we would expect also that the national executives would show spiritual maturity, but here is where the missionary can show the way. If others are small or ambitious, and fail to manifest the right attitude, let the missionary give the example of what true Christian leadership is. There are no restrictions to abounding in love!

5

Missionary Relationships

THE MISSIONARY FIELD STRUCTURE

The term "Field Fellowship" or "Missionary
Field Council" refers to the approved structure
for the coordinated effort among missionaries on
a given field in foreign lands. It will soon
become apparent to the new missionary that work
on the mission field is different than in the
homeland. Most new missionaries have come from
a background of a pastorate. The question of
close cooperation with his fellow ministers was
not too important. He could do his work in his
own church and let the other man carry out his
own program in his church.

The problem is complicated on the mission
field because, at least to a measure, we work
with the same people. What one missionary does
affects every other missionary on the field.
For example, if one missionary feels as a matter
of principle that he should be conservative in
the matter of handing out funds to nationals,

and he considers this important in the building of the national church, he will be dismayed and feel frustrated if his fellow missionaries do not share these same ideals and hand out money freely. Not only so, but it will not be too long before the nationals begin to make comparison of one missionary with another and measure their appreciation for the missionary by the amount of money that he distributes. Thus, one man's generosity makes another man appear to be stingy and unloving.

THE INDIVIDUAL AND THE TEAM

In a team effort, who makes the point is not as important as the winning of the game. Every player must subject his own personal will and desires to the good of the game. First Corinthians, chapter 12 gives us an even higher concept of cooperation. There we are compared to members of a body working together under one Head.

Probably every individual missionary has a primary concern for the success of his own ministry. This is really, however, only a part of the picture. Three things must be brought into line for a satisfactory team effort on the mission field. The missionary must work with his fellow missionaries, and the missionaries as a group must work with the church and with the national organization that governs that church. Finally, the missionary's own particular call and ministry must be satisfied.

The missionary's own personal abilities and ministries, and the situation of his family should be taken into account. Health problems must sometimes be considered in regard to the location of a missionary. While it perhaps should not be the determining factor, yet

schooling for the missionaries' children also
becomes an important factor in the location of a
missionary family. All of these considerations
contribute to making missionary work a most
complex activity today. Missionaries must
strive to remember that they are not simply
individuals, but are members of a body.

Rivalry should be unknown in the work of God.
However, missionaries, like God's people every-
where, have not yet attained their true stature
in Christ. Consequently, rivalries and selfishness are manifested among missionaries. Some
seem to want to build a kingdom for themselves,
instead of building the Kingdom of God. Perhaps
this is unconscious in many cases. We can hide
selfishness behind our "zeal for the Lord".
Someone has pointed out that the ministry
affords an ideal situation for developing selfishness. It sometimes takes the form of ambition for office, sometimes that of having a more
shining report for the folks at home. We have
seen missionaries become upset because their
supporting churches were contacted by the
mission office for help on a project in their
country, but which did not particularly benefit
their own area. The question of which missionary has the better housing or furniture can
evoke envy on the part of some.

How important it is for missionaries to
remember that they are not rivals, but partners
in the work of the Lord! We are a body, and if
one member prospers, we should rejoice with him,
rather than being envious of the harvest that
he was able to reap. As members of the same
body, no one can rob us of our place if we
exercise faith, humility and obedience to God.
How often has the work of God been hindered
because His servants did not hold these truths
in proper perspective.

THE INDIVIDUAL AND BODY MINISTRY

We now come to the difficult problem of harmonizing individual initiative with the concept of body ministry. Some persons in a reaction to ecclesiastical machinery and bondage have insisted that they take their orders individually from the Head of the Church. It is probable that too many of us think of our ministry in the terms of a modern Samson or an Elijah. We tend to forget that we are living in a new era and that the highest norm of ministry in the New Testament is body ministry. This is emphasized over and over again in the teaching of the epistles.

A good example of the solution to this problem can be found in the life of Paul himself. He received his call at the time of his conversion (Acts 9). In Galatians 2 we are told that he conferred not with flesh and blood, but went to Arabia and received the revelation of the gospel that he preached. He goes so far as to say that Peter and John, pillars in the church, added nothing to him.

However, in the actual carrying out of his ministry, we see him waiting for God's time and for the approval of the church. This came when the Holy Spirit said, "Separate me Paul and Barnabas for the work where unto I have called them" (Acts 13:1-4). They were already called, but they needed the confirmation and the backing of the church. Note, too, that Paul states that he was commanded by God to go up to Jerusalem (Galatians 2:1-3), and lay before the brethren his doctrine that he preached among the Gentiles, "lest I had run in vain." Paul, who without doubt knew that his revelation was from God, yet realized that he must also submit to his brethren. Otherwise, there might have been two

Christian churches in the beginning: the
Pauline church and the Jerusalem church. Paul
could afford to submit his divine revelation for
the approval of his brethren. He trusted the
Holy Spirit to illuminate them. We are on safe
ground in seeking that the church endorse our
individual guidance and ministry.

THE ORGANIZATION OF A FIELD FELLOWSHIP

It is logical for missionaries sent out by
the same board to the same area to organize some
kind of a field fellowship or field council.
Otherwise, every missionary will be left to his
own devices and there will be no coordination of
evangelism or other projects.

In reading the account of Paul's missionary
journey in the book of Acts, it becomes apparent
that at first Barnabas was the leader, and that
later Paul became the head of the missionary
band that accompanied him, and he coordinated
the activities of the team. The members did not
operate independently of one another. When John
Mark returned home without the approval of the
leaders, he was subject to censure (Acts 12:25;
13:5,13; 15:37-39).

In much the same way, each missionary coming
to the field with the approval of the home
office must understand that he must cooperate
with field leadership and form a part of the
team. He is not to take his own initiative in
promoting projects and raising money for them
among his supporting churches, or appoint
workers on his own to follow up his campaigns.
Such matters affect other missionaries and if
there is a national organization it is also
involved.

The field fellowship should be organized with its own chairman and officers, and have a simple constitution to guide it in its operation. Decisions should be reached in a proper manner, with all members having the opportunity of expressing their opinion.

Every missionary granted appointment automatically becomes a member of the Field Fellowship. In a well-organized missionary effort, there is no such thing as a missionary appointed to a field who is not also a member of the Field Fellowship. The missionary program cannot be run by remote control. For the home office to handle each problem separately without reference to field leadership would only bring confusion.

The Field Fellowship is the structure through which the missionary effort can be coordinated with the national church and with the missionary team. It is important then that the missionary understand his relationship to the Field Fellowship and to the national work. It is understood that decisions made by the Field Fellowship are subject to review by the home board.

Business-like procedures should be followed in the session of the Missionary Field Fellowship. When business is to be taken up, an agenda should be made with each missionary having the opportunity of putting items on the agenda which he believes should be discussed. Then the chairman should bring up the items on the agenda one by one, leaving ample room for discussion. The decision should be reached by a motion and a vote should be taken and the decision recorded in the minutes.

During the time that the Field Fellowship is not in session, certain responsibilities will be placed in the hands of the Executive Field

Fellowship Committee. These officers are to
take care of business for the Field Fellowship
under the guidelines that the Field Fellowship
has set forth. Such decisions made must be
reported back to the Field Fellowship in the
next meeting. Financial reports are given so
that the members of the Field Fellowship know
how the finances have been handled.

The Field Fellowship has responsibilities to
the Foreign Missions Board and to the national
church. The officers of the Field Fellowship
should be chosen on the basis of mature judgment
and capabilities. It should not be a matter
simply of personal preference. The chairmanship
should not be shifted from one missionary to
another every year. Missionary leadership on
the field should have an opportunity to develop.
The Field Fellowship needs to engage in long-
range planning. This cannot be done when there
is a constant shift of executive personnel.

THE IMPORTANCE OF ATTITUDES

As members of a field fellowship, personal
attitudes are important. Individual missionaries must keep in mind the total objectives of
the field. A missionary's interests should go
beyond his own individual activity and sphere.
There should also be concern for the success of
fellow missionaries. We should do our best to
help them to succeed. This is particularly true
in the relationship of older missionaries to
younger missionaries. The Field Chairman and
the committee have a responsibility to young
missionaries.

The sending board also should become
involved in insuring the success of new missionaries and do everything possible to help them
overcome the obstacles that they may face. Some

have found that it is helpful to set up an evaluation program for new missionaries during their
probationary term as first-termers. The purpose
of the evaluation is not judgmental, but correc-
tive, with the idea of giving the new missionary
a chance to correct mistakes before he comes to
the end of his term. If older missionaries will
take the Christ-like attitude that Barnabas took
with Paul in order to help him get started in
his ministry, they will be doing a service to
the body of Christ (Acts 9:26-29; 11:25; 26).

On the other side of the coin, the new missionaries should not be quick to discount the
labor and effort that has gone into the work up
to that point. It is a common failure of all
of us to see weaknesses rather than strong
points. There have been first-term missionaries
with less than a year's experience on the field
who have roundly criticized the older missionaries, stating that things were not being done
correctly. Actually they should have been
listening and learning, rather than passing
judgments. Perhaps the young missionary may be
correct in his assessments, but the probabili-
ties are that given a little more time, and
more insight into the problems faced on the
field, the criticism would be less caustic and
more sympathetic and constructive. Younger
missionaries should show appreciation for the
effort of those who have gone before them.
Someone has said, "Youth is like a child born
in the night who sees the sunrise and thinks
that there never was a yesterday."

Missionaries, whether junior or senior,
should learn to trust one another. Give the
benefit of the doubt to the other person. We
must try to put ourselves in the other person's
shoes and remember that people do not have to
be perfect in order to have our love. Let us

make room for each other in our hearts. When we help each other, we help ourselves, and we help the body of Christ.

The Field Fellowship should not be just a time of business dealing with the problems that confront the missionary family, but it should also be a time of warm spiritual fellowship. Let not the area of prayer fellowship be neglected in the meetings. Rather let missionaries pray for one another, and love one another and help one another. It has proved profitable to set aside a full day for spiritual fellowship, encouragement and prayer in the yearly meeting before the items of business are taken up.

6

The Overseas Church and Missionary Finance

The matter of church finance is closely
related to the previous chapter on the missionaries' partnership with the national church.
The case for a church which supports its own
ministry and depends upon its own financial
resources has been presented in detail in the
author's books.* Here we will merely summarize
the dangers of depending on foreign funds and
the benefits of self-support for the purpose
of providing a proper background for decisions
that must be made in the present situation.

IMPORTANCE OF SELF-SUPPORT

The danger of depending on foreign support
for salaries of pastors and the maintenance of
the work may be itemized as follows:

The Indigenous Church and *Build My Church*
(Gospel Publishing House), and *Growing Young
Churches* (Moody Press).

*These other books are not
in print but may be in*

There is a danger to the church itself. Sometimes instead of helping, subsidy often destroys the very principle that will produce a strong vital church. It has been amply demonstrated that for a church to depend upon foreign sources for its finances kills its initiative and deadens the sense of responsibility.

We might draw a comparison from those wild animals that have been found in time of infancy by nature-loving people and raised in the shelter of their home. The animal is deprived of the hardships of the struggle for existence, and if it must revert to its natural state, it may perish either from lack of sufficient food, or because it has not learned to defend itself against its natural enemies. Or, like the sea gulls of the Gulf coast that learned to depend upon the shrimp boats to provide them food from the refuse of the catch, they finally became so dependent upon the fishing fleet that when it was removed, the gulls did not know how to fend for themselves and perished. An old proverb says, "Give a man a fish and you help him for a day; teach him to fish and you help him for the rest of his life."

One has only to look at the strong indigenous evangelical churches in certain sections of the world to see a demonstration of the fact that churches do better when they learn to depend upon their own resources. In some cities missions are struggling with small congregations with mission-paid pastors, and the congregations have had their churches built for them with foreign funds. In those same cities, there are large congregations that in the midst of the same poverty, usually without foreign help from abroad, have built large church buildings and are carrying on a vital and rapidly expanding

evangelistic program. Surely this should say
something to us.

The second danger is to the worker himself.
We develop when our faith is put to the test.
Struggle and sacrifice have their part in the
development of every man of God. God has His
own way of maturing workers which is often
thwarted when we supply artificial help from
foreign funds. The worker learns to depend upon
the mission instead of upon God. This is also
a cause of deep conflicts between missionaries
and national workers since rarely does the
mission have enough funds at its disposal to
actually pay the worker an adequate salary.
Tensions that are produced result in anti-
missionary feeling.

This brings us to another vital point. If
the church in a given country is dependent upon
mission funds, it goes without saying that *the
work cannot advance any further than the supply
line will permit*. The limit to expansion is
imposed by the limitation of funds. This is an
impossible situation for the Church of Jesus
Christ. In this day when the nations of the
world are demanding to exercise complete freedom
from foreign domination, it is an anachronism
for the church to be placed in a situation
where the possibility of its advance is dicated
by the amount of foreign funds available.

Also the subsidizing of a church by a foreign mission *projects the public image of a
foreign-dominated work*. If the church is to
grow, it must be seen as something that, by its
inherent nature, can grow in any culture.
Foreign missions support will project the
opposite image. The Church is seen in such
cases as the introduction of a foreign religion,
and often related to imperial domination. No

matter how earnestly and honestly the mission
may desire that the church expand in its own
right, the fact that the money for the support
of the church comes from the foreign mission
carries with it the idea of control. The
nationals realize that the mission could cut
off its support at any time. The church does
not have true freedom to make its own decisions
when its very existence depends on foreign
funds.

A somewhat subtle argument for foreign
support of overseas churches has been brought
forward and emphasized recently. The Church is
one, it is said, and the Church in different
areas has different needs. If one country
needs personnel, then perhaps a teacher or an
evangelist could be sent. The church that has
such individuals should share them with the
church that does not have them. In some countries the church has personnel but does not have
the finances to support them. The church that
has the finances should supply funds to the
church that is lacking them. We cannot accept
this argument without qualifications. To do so
would be to overlook other important factors.

It is true that the Church is one and what
is lacking in one area may be supplied from
another part of the body. However, we do
violence to the concept of the responsibility
of the members of the body of Christ if we
interpret this to mean that certain members are
thereby excused from doing what they rightfully
should do. For example, the fact that one
church in one country may have a good evangelist, and can supply an evangelistic ministry to
another church, does not relieve the receiving
church from evangelizing. It must still
carry its own responsibility in soul winning.
Likewise, the fact that one church may have

more financial resources than another church
does not mean that the poorer church is relieved
of its responsibility of paying tithes and
supporting its own minister. The generosity of
one church should not be an excuse for another
church to fail to fulfill its responsibilities.
Louis King at the Green Lake Missions Executive
Conference said, "No church can successfully
assume another church's obligation to Biblical
faith, life and mission" (Wagner 1972).

The benefits to a church that finds its own
resources for its maintenance and expansion are
thus evident. The church is likely to be more
vital, more alive, and more responsible.
Further, there is no limit to the amount of
expansion that can be experienced. The minister
can enjoy the freedom of exercising faith in God
for his support rather than depending on a
mission.

A SENSE OF RESPONSIBILITY

All of this does not mean that there is never
a time that foreign funds should be used to
stimulate or help the work of God overseas.
There are times and places where outside money
can be helpful. It is the missionaries' task to
determine when financial aid will strengthen or
weaken the church. *A sense of responsibility* is
a "pearl of great price" in the overseas church
and its ministry. The overseas church must be a
church in its own right, never a second class
church that can not govern itself, support
itself, or develop its own ministries. Anything
that a missionary does to help this church to
realize its true mission is in order. Everything
that he does that diminishes this sense of responsibility and makes the church more dependent
upon him or his organization is a sin against
the church. So, if he will ask himself the

question, "Will this gift make this church more
dependent on me or the mission, or will it help
the church to realize its own identity under God
and function as a true church?", then this will
serve as a criterion to determine where and how
help should be given. A word of warning: let
us not reach the conclusion too quickly that the
church is unable to assume financial responsibility. The church when thrown back on its own
resources will often do that which missionaries
have thought could not be done.

Basically, mission help should be given to
help the church attain its goals. Mission help
should never be a *substitute* for self-help. The
mission should not do for a church what it is
unwilling to do for itself. This is why self-
support and self-government are so closely
aligned. The process of decision-making is
important to the assuming of responsibility.

Further, the missionary must distinguish
between short-term and long-term benefits. It
is entirely possible that a gift of money may
prove to be of temporary benefit, but may in
the long run tend to make the church dependent.
For example: the construction of a church
building with foreign funds may result in
immediate growth and increase, but at the cost
of engendering expectations on the part of
other congregations that their building will
also be provided for them. Why should they
struggle and sacrifice, if by patiently waiting
the missionary will arrange to have it built
for them?

It would seem to be in order for financial
help to be given in the training program to prepare ministers for the fulfilling of their
vocation. Also, it is logical to help provide
a building as a base for a church in a large

city where the cost of property is so high that
it is completely beyond the reach of the local
congregation. Even so, this help should be
given in such a way that it will not become a
"missions project". The local congregation
should be expected to assume its responsibility
and make the sacrifices to construct the building, understanding that the mission is giving
them a boost to help them on their way, but is
not doing the job for them.

CHURCH PROPERTIES

The question of how properties will be held
becomes an important question. In these days
when most countries have restrictions about
foreign-held properties, it would seem to be
the part of wisdom to turn as many church
properties over to the national organization as
possible. Probably Bible institute properties
will be the last to be transferred to the
national organization. However, there is no
reason that this should not be done once the
national organization has reached a state of
maturity and experience in fiscal matters to
insure proper handling. In some cases because
of local laws, the national organization has
become the owner of these properties from the
very beginning, and this has not usually
resulted in problems.

Missions would do well to hold loosely to
the material aspects of their missionary
endeavor. Properties, like individuals, are
expendable. It is the Church that must go on.

7

The Missionary and Evangelism

Evangelism is the very heart of the missionary
ministry. Evangelism is what missionary work is
all about. Propagation of the gospel is, of the
three basic factors of the indigenous church,
the most important.

THE GOAL OF EVANGELISM

Evangelism needs a definition. Self-propaga-
tion as it relates to the Church is a little
more definitive. When we speak of evangelism we
are not referring simply to handing out literature or preaching on a street corner, although
these may be included in evangelistic activities.
Evangelism includes, *first*, the proclamation of
the gospel to the unconverted; *second*, the per-
suading of men to accept Christ and to come to a
personal relationship with him; *third*, helping
these converts to find their place as members of
a local church. In the New Testament example
and teaching, there seems to be no place for
simply making converts without relating them to

local churches. The work of evangelism is not terminated until converts have found their place as functioning members of the body of Christ.

In the pioneer stages of missionary work, the missionary's contribution to evangelism is self-evident. This is what he went to do: preach the gospel, win men to Christ, and form churches. Later when some churches have already been formed, and perhaps there is a national organization serving these churches, the question arises, "What can the missionary now do toward the main objective of evangelism?"

TWO-FOLD MISSIONARY CONTRIBUTION

The missionary's contribution to evangelism falls naturally in two parts: first, that which he can do himself as an individual minister and Christian to win men to Christ; and second, what he can do by teaching and inspiring others, thus stimulating the churches to carry out their evangelistic ministry.

There is an all too common tendency for missionaries to become less and less involved personally in evangelism. When the missionary first goes to a field, evangelism is his primary responsibility; his efforts are expended mainly in traveling to new areas--the opening of preaching points, and in personal witness and persuasion. As the years go by, he finds it constantly more difficult to engage in his primary ministry. Many things crowd in. There is the administrative work of the mission, the teaching in the Bible school, the special conferences--so that in the end he may find that very little of his time is given to presenting Christ to the unconverted. The missionary must continually make a conscious effort to correct this. We must not forget that

we are called to reconcile men to God. Let
every missionary strive constantly in prayer and
seek the help of the Spirit to keep this vision
and ministry alive.

AVENUES OF MISSIONARY EVANGELISM

There is, of course, a distinct possibility
that a missionary may continue in his primary
evangelistic ministry, even after there are
churches formed and a national organization is
functioning. Actually, there is no reason for
believing that a national organization is prepared immediately to assume the total responsibility of evangelism with all that this involves.

Usually, even though the national organization is formed, the churches exist in only
certain sections of the country. There will be
entire states or provinces without any church
and perhaps others with only one or two. Now,
this presents an opportunity for the continuance
of missionary ministry. And happily enough,
this is normally what the national church
desires the missionary to do. In my experience,
the anti-missionary feeling has developed
particularly in those areas where missionaries
are clustered in the capital, or larger cities,
rather than getting out into the outlying
departments and establishing churches.

There are, of course, many reasons why
missionary families stay in the capital cities.
One is that they are often required to teach in
the Bible institute. Another very important
consideration is the education of the missionary
children. Often the schooling available is not
adequate in the outlying districts, and to go
outside of the capital city means that the
missionary must undertake to teach his own
children or else send them away to a boarding

school. Naturally, these are alternatives that
many times are unacceptable to a missionary, and
so he stays in the capital.

Many things determine the decision. When the
country is small geographically, it may be that
the capital provides ready access to every
section of the country, and nothing would really
be gained by moving out to a smaller town. At
other times the family situation is such that
the choice is either to stay in the capital, or
withdraw temporarily from missionary service in
order to place the children in school. The
general policy of some missions requires that
parents send their children to boarding school
when they reach a certain age so that the parents may be free to minister in the area of
greatest need. This is often harder on the
parents than on the children, and while there
are exceptions, the sending of children away to
boarding school has not had unfavorable conse-
quences as a general rule. We do not attempt at
this point to generalize or give directions to
missionary families. We simply point out that
often there are opportunities to go out into the
provinces. When a family has pre-school children, the parents are still free to live in more
isolated surroundings. Also, the missionaries
whose children have already left home could
return again to this type of ministry. Others
will find a way to give their children the
needed schooling and move to an outlying department. What is important here is the motivation
and the vision.

After fifteen years of missionary service, it
is easy to allow secondary considerations to
deprive us of our primary missionary ministry.
In the beginning of a missionary ministry, there
is often willingness to make very real sacrifices to see the work progress. It does not

necessarily follow, because we started this way,
that this same level of consecration and dedica-
tion will continue. It requires the continual
work of the Holy Spirit in our hearts to keep us
alert and alive to the opportunities and
challenges before us.

Another way that a missionary may help in
evangelism is through conducting campaigns in
the larger cities. This will, of course, depend
upon whether he has an evangelistic ministry.
He may do this himself, as an evangelist, or he
may simply be the man who inspires and arranges
for the evangelistic campaigns.

National church leaders have a point when
they say that the missionary has facilities for
evangelistic and pioneer work that they do not
have. Often he has a car and public address
systems. Sometimes he either has a tent or
could secure one. He may have funds available
to rent an auditorium. Above all, he has
mobility, which is something that the national
may lack, and which may multiply his difficulties. In no sense is this an excuse for
nationals not getting into active evangelistic
work and pioneering new areas. However, if the
national pastors see the missionary with all of
his equipment and abilities staying in the city
and seemingly indifferent to evangelism, it has
an adverse effect upon the national's vision.
Why should he make sacrifices that men of
supposedly greater consecration, ability, and
with more facilities, fail to make?

Campaigns in the city do not necessarily
require a building. A tent is very useful, and
in the absence of this, an open lot in a dry
season can be very productive. It does not cost
too much to erect a temporary platform, string
some lights up, connect public address systems,

and invite the public to an open-air meeting.
At least in Latin America, hundreds will come to
an open-air meeting that would not think of
going into a Protestant church. Dozens and perhaps hundreds of churches have been started in
this manner.

EVANGELISM BY TEACHING

The second part of the missionary's contribution in encouraging evangelism and self-propaga-
tion is in what he can do through others by
teaching and guiding his national brethren.

One of the greater ministries that is open
today to missionaries working with the national
church is that of teaching among the churches.
Many of the churches need to be inspired with
vision for the evangelizing of their neighbor-
hood. We all have seen comparatively small
congregations of 100 or 200 people happily
content in a section of a large city with
perhaps a half-million inhabitants, making no
real effort to reach the city. They work with
the relatives of the members, with the friends
they bring to the services, or with the
strangers that may drop in during a campaign,
and they feel that they have done their duty.
Perhaps ten blocks away, not one in five people
know that the church exists.

To make matters worse, sometimes the pastor
of the church will object to another effort
being made in the city, feeling that he has a
franchise on the whole city. This is a deplor-
able situation that needs to be corrected.
Missionaries can make a valuable contribution to
such churches by imparting to them the vision of
winning a lost world for Christ. He can further
show them methods by which the church can reach
out. We have often emphasized that every church

is responsible for all the territory around, at least half way to the next church.

Recently, in a medium-sized city, one of the pastors came to a missionary* who was emphasizing the ministry of the lay members and said to him, "What can I do? I have about sixty members, and I have been preaching to them for about two years. We seldom see an outsider in the church, and very few people are converted in our services. We have services every night of the week. There are Bible studies and young peoples' meetings, women's meetings, etc." The missionary replied, "Close down your services for two weeks, except on Sundays. Get your members to invite you to a different home every night of the week. Have them invite their neighbors and friends to a house meeting. Then go from place to place during the week. Invite tham all to come in to church on Sunday." After two weeks the national pastor reported to the missionary, "Can you believe it? I have preached to 68 new people in these two weeks, more new people than I have preached to in the church in two years."

Branch Sunday Schools provide another way to reach out into the community. In one Central American city, one church with about 80 members trained 25 Sunday school workers, and at one given time reached 2,000 people over one weekend. Sunday school classes were held in homes of believers, and even in the homes of the unconverted. Some classes were held in a park under trees!

Every Christian is a witness for Jesus Christ. God expects every converted person to tell what

---

*
Reported by Arthur Lindvall, an Assemblies of God missionary to Latin America.

he has found in Jesus. To witness is a
natural result of having met Christ. When the
love of God fills a person's heart, he wants to
tell others about it. There is usually an
absence of inhibitions in the newly converted
Christian. He wants to share. The problem is
that the newly converted Christian often sees
older Christians who seemingly are unconcerned
or indifferent about spreading the gospel. He
learns from them, quenches the Spirit, and
finally becomes just another church member sit-
ting in the pew, not really involved in God's
work. Often the missionary can show a better
way and the church can establish a different
pattern.

We have elsewhere explained how a church can
fill the area with preaching points, using lay
members to carry on this work. Some of these
preaching points should develop into churches
which will continue to spread the gospel and
establish other preaching points and churches.
Actually, it is better to have twenty smaller
churches with 100 members each, scattered
throughout the city, than to have one great
church with 2,000 members. Both are important,
and we do not underrate the big church with its
appeal and ministry to a class of people that
the small church will not reach. But, block by
block, and individual by individual, several
smaller churches are more likely to do the job
of total evangelism in a city. Happily, there
is a place for both large and small churches.

Every church should consider itself a mother
church and seek to establish daughter churches
throughout the area. It is a tragedy when the
vision of the church becomes inverted so that
the members think only of their own needs and of
maintaining their own program. Some pastors are
quite content to carry on with the church as

long as the offerings are sufficient to pay
their salary. They feel that in maintaining the
church, they are discharging their duty. The
missionary may help to inspire pastors and
churches with the vision of total evangelism.

LAY WORKERS TRAINING

Another area of need in the carrying out of
this evangelistic outreach is the training of
the lay workers who will be going to take care
of the preaching points. The pastor of each
church may give some training, but the pastor
himself often needs help to know how to teach
these budding workers. The missionary would do
well to prepare courses that the pastors may
teach to their own workers. This would include
the subjects such as "How to Direct a Service",
"The Standards of Christian Living", "Prayer",
"House-to-House Evangelism", etc. In fact, the
missionary himself can move among the churches
with courses of this nature. If the situation
permits, several churches could come together
for a couple of weeks of study. Perhaps there
is no greater contribution that a missionary can
make than this teaching ministry to local
churches. This effort is further explained in
the following chapter under the heading "Teaching for Christian Maturity."

The missionary who is called upon to teach in
a Bible school can have a powerful influence on
the students by presenting the vision and
methods for evangelism. He must, however, have
a heart filled with evangelistic fervor. It is
not enough to present the material in a methodi-
cal manner simply with the objective that the
students get a good grade on their examinations.
The teacher must have the fire of evangelism in
his soul. He should also lead the way by
example. The Bible school is vital in the

development of the national church, since the students who go through the school will normally be the leaders of the church in the future. How important it is then that the Bible school not simply be a place to learn theory, but where the students are inspired and led in this primary ministry of winning souls and establishing churches.

The time spent in Bible School should not only be a time for acquiring knowledge, but also for practical work in evangelism. The students should not lose contact with the world around them. Weekends should be spent as far as possible in evangelistic activities.

EVANGELISTIC CENTERS

Beginning some twenty-five years ago, there was a move toward establishing great evangelistic centers, especially in the large cities. Usually, it was thought of these in terms of being a center for large campaigns. A bookstore, a radio program, and perhaps a night school for Bible training was to be a part of the regular activities for the evangelistic center. It was not anticipated that this evangelistic center would develop into a church, but that it would become the center from which converts could go out and establish churches throughout the city. Experience has proved that in general, these evangelistic centers usually become large churches and operate as such.

There are some problems in regard to the concept of an evangelistic center. For one thing, if it is envisioned that a missionary will be in control with national helpers for over an indefinite period of time, this inevitably produces some areas of tension within the national organization, for the evangelistic center can easily become a sort of missionary island within the national organization.

How does the evangelistic center fit into the national organization? In order to give continuity to its ministry, and to meet the financial obligation, it is necessary to have regular membership. The center needs the financial support of the people. So the evangelistic center becomes their church home. Thus, at times a church has been brought into existence whose relationship with the rest of the churches is not too clear.

Another problem is the fact that people who go out from evangelistic centers as workers do not really have sufficient experience in the operation of a regular church, unless the evangelistic center engages in a church planting ministry. They know how to run an evangelistic center, but not a church!

Probably one of the biggest problems has been the fact that the missionaries who have been in charge of the evangelistic centers have developed a different type of program than is carried on by the local churches. Many of the outside visitors, such as renowned evangelists, in coming to the city, came to the evangelistic center and bypassed the little churches. This caused some resentment. Also, when the evangelistic center holds a big meeting, the other churches feel that it attracts the people away from their own churches.

Not the least of the problems lies in *when* and *how* to make an evangelistic center "indigenous". The difference between the level of a missionary's ministry and that of the national brother has sometimes been too great to bridge.

Some of the advantages of the evangelistic center are:

(1) An evangelistic center is usually made to accommodate a much larger group of people and gives a sense of stability to the work.

(2) The people of better class in the community are likely to find themselves more at home in an evangelistic center with its larger congregation and an atmosphere more congenial to their culture.

(3) When the evangelistic center has remained faithful to its purpose, it has often been the means of starting other churches throughout the city.

So much depends on the leadership and clearly outlined, long-range goals. It is evident that the plan to run the evangelistic center without its being a church is not practical. The church formed in the center should submit to all the rules and regulations of the national organization. A clearly outlined constitution showing its relationship to the national organization will be helpful. Open communications are absolutely necessary.

One of the most successful operations of an evangelistic center that has come to the writer's attention is that of San Salvador, capital of El Salvador, Central America. It was established in a time of evangelistic outreach in the city, and there were about twelve other small churches of the same denomination in the city at the time of its founding. For one regular Sunday in May of 1975, the Sunday school report on attendance read as follows:

In the Evangelistic Center itself	890
In the outstations of the Evangelistic Center	2,877
In the 8 annexes related to the Evangelistic Center	9,029
TOTAL	12,680

Certain factors have contributed to the growth and stability of this Evangelistic Center:

(1) The Evangelistic Center has a clear agreement with the national church body.

(2) The director of the Evangelistic Center is a Spanish-American missionary, raised by missionary parents in Latin America. His acceptance is that of a Latin American.

(3) The church supports two co-pastors. The director is gradually withdrawing from the Center, to leave it more completely in the hands of the national ministers.

(4) There is a large day school with over a thousand students which covers the entire area from primary through high school. This school is sponsored by the Evangelistic Center but is largely self-supporting. The school provides a channel of contact with many families otherwise unreached by the gospel.

(5) The director has fired the congregation with the challenge of discipleship and evangelism.

(6) The outstation system, so fruitful in Central America, has been used by the Evagnelistic Center with profit with an addition.

(7) The outstations stay for a longer period of time under the umbrella of the Evangelistic Center. The Evangelistic Center provides them first with a rented house or hall, and one of the local lay preachers of the Evangelistic Center becomes the pastor, while still retaining his employment. The Evangelistic Center endeavors to help each outstation (at this stage called an annex) to secure its own building. Then the annex can move toward autonomy, supporting its own pastor, and finally being set in order as an autonomous church of the national organization. One has been thus organized and others are in the process. It is felt that by not severing the ties with the mother church too quickly, it gives a certain security to the young church, and also a sense of belonging to a successful evangelical community.

ENCOURAGING MISSIONS

Finally, missionaries should lead the churches in a vision for missions beyond their country. Missionaries have gone out to foreign fields because of the missionary vision that others passed on to them. Certainly they have not waited until all the cities were evangelized in their homeland before they went out. Why then should they wait until the whole country is reached by the gospel before they present to them the challenge of carrying the gospel to the ends of the earth?

Admittedly, there are problems, one of the chief of which is the lack of finances. Yet we know that churches in the U.S.A., which also have great needs themselves, take up regular missionary offerings to send the gospel abroad. Do we do well when we withhold this vision and challenge from the churches overseas?

Happily, in some areas of the world, the national church has already begun to send out missionaries--sometimes to neighboring tribes, sometimes to neighboring countries, and occasionally across the sea. Some national churches have already formed missions departments. This is to be encouraged. The missionary would do well to resurrect some of the missionary sermons he preached to the churches at home and preach them again to the younger churches overseas.

Let us pass on the torch of world evangelism which we ourselves have received, and the vision which impelled us to go to the regions beyond, to the national churches so that every church and every individual may truly feel himself a part of the world-wide outreach of the universal Church.

8

Initiating Services for the National church

As the national church develops, new and pressing needs call for attention. Opportunities
present themselves that require all of the
ingenuity and strength of missionaries and
nationals alike to be able to bring the almost
unlimited possibilities to fruition. Some of
the more pressing needs are:

1. Advanced education for national leaders
   and Bible institute teachers.

2. Maturation of the Christians in the
   national churches.

3. Literature for the unsaved, the Christian, the pastor, and textbooks for
   Bible institutes.

4. Some plan and activity of evangelism
   that will inspire and mobilize the
   church to reach the unevangelized
   areas of the country.

In the period of the writer's administrative
work in Latin America, programs to help meet
these needs began to be developed. One of the
first and important steps was the bringing
together of national leadership in the various
countries of Latin America for area conferences
in which the needs of the work could be discussed with missionaries and nationals. Since
Latin America extends over such a wide area, we
finally broke these area conferences down into
three sections: 1) the southern section of
South America; 2) the northern section of South
America with Middle America; and 3) the West
Indies. Such conferences were aided in Latin
America by the fact that we had main languages
in which to work. Spanish was the language of
the bulk of the countries. The large country of
Brazil spoke the Portuguese language. The West
Indies were divided among English, Spanish, and
French. However, the problem was complicated by
the fact that many of these areas were in
different stages of development. Hence, their
needs were different.

PROGRAM OF CHRISTIAN EDUCATION

About the time that the area conferences
were being initiated, an effort was made to
evaluate our Bible institute work for the preparation of pastors. Several men and women
prominent in Bible school work were brought
together and spent six weeks evaluating the
programs. There had been in Latin America wide
divergence in the Bible institute programs since
these grew out of the initiative of the missionaries involved. Schools ran for different
lengths of time and different subjects were
taught. Some were fairly sophisticated and
others were quite simple.

From this study, a basic plan for Bible schools evolved which was to become the basis of evaluation for Bible schools throughout Latin America. In our area conferences, special committees composed of national leaders and missionaries were formed for the purpose of encouraging Christian education in the different national churches. Finally, the new Bible school committees working in the Spanish area together with representatives from the Portuguese area met for intensive study of the Bible institute situation, and approved the Basic Plan as a guide to all of our Latin American schools. This guide was not imposed upon the schools in the different countries, but was presented as a service and tool for evaluation. In fact, the Basic Plan has such flexibility that it can serve as a guide to schools with different lengths of sessions, for day or night schools, and also makes room for studies by correspondence. A missionary was named by the Missions board to serve as coordinator of the Christian education program in Latin America and to help implement the Basic Plan in the different schools when such help was requested.

Advanced Leadership Training

After the Basic Plan had been accepted, the next need to capture the attention of the joint committee was the need for training of national leaders, such as superintendents and Bible school teachers. It was quite evidently impossible for such leaders to get their training by going to the United States or some other far-removed area. The superintendents were continually occupied, as were the Bible school teachers, so that they could not afford to take leave for a whole year from their respective responsibilities. This ruled out not only the sending of students abroad, but the establishing

of a school in some given point in Latin America
for the training of leaders. It was recognized
that to establish a regular campus and require
that the students attend from a distance, even
though the financial problems could be solved,
yet the student body would certainly be limited
to younger, unattached men and the leaders now
occupying prominent posts who needed the training would not be helped.

The solution reached by the committee was to
divide all of Latin America and the West Indies
into several sections with a system of month-
long class sessions followed by two years of
correspondence work. The plan called for three
such month-long sessions, and a total of four
years of correspondence work. To do this, it
was necessary to develop a roving faculty which
could go from area to area and implement the
courses of study.

Records of each student are kept in a central
office and the work done corresponds to univer-
sity or seminary level. Three categories of
recognition for completion of the course are
granted: a certificate for those who complete
the entire course satisfactorily but may not
have completed all of their work as required by
the Basic Plan for institutes; a diploma for
those who complete this advanced work and have
also graduated from a Bible institute; and
finally, a degree for those who have received a
bachelor degree for academic work, having
finished also the Bible institute work and
completed the advanced seminary work.

This system has proved very satisfactory at
the present stage of development of the work.
This is evidenced by the fact that there are
over 800 pastors and leaders enrolled in the
courses at the present time. It is, however,

very demanding work for those that direct the
program. The system requires much travel, and
long absences from home. However, the results
are proving to be satisfactory and missionaries
engaged in this type of work are making an
important contribution to the national churches
in general. It should be noted that while at
the present time the administration of this
program and most of the teachers are missionaries, yet the plan calls for involving an ever-
increasing number of national ministers as
teachers. Several such national ministers have
already taught courses in the program.

One of the greatest advantages of this system
is that it grew out of the conference with the
national leaders themselves, and they do not
feel that the program has the stamp of "made in
the U.S.A." on it. The nationals are enthusiastic supporters of this Program of Advanced
Christian Education.

TEACHING FOR CHRISTIAN MATURITY

The next need that came into focus was the
teaching of church members in the area of Christian development and maturity. In many
churches the Christian teaching has largely been
limited to elementary teaching given to new converts to prepare them for baptism. It was felt
that pastors needed to engage in a teaching
ministry that would cover the area of Christian
maturity, evangelism, and church extension. For
this purpose, the elementary Bible course was
developed. Originally, it contained ten small
books which were eventually combined into three
volumes with the idea that the pastor could
teach his congregation a series of studies each
year which might continue for three years.

This program has proved to be highly successful. In the first place, it puts materials in
the hands of pastors which help them to develop
their teaching ministry. Secondly, it provides
much-needed teaching for the Christians to
foster their spiritual development; and third,
it helps the church in its outreach as it gives
training for house-to-house visitation and helps
the lay preacher as he takes care of his outstation. In some countries the national church
has made the teaching of this course a national
project for the pastors and churches. The
results have been most gratifying and new
churches have developed as a result of this
activity.

Missionaries can find a most fruitful ministry by sponsoring this type of studies among the
churches. One missionary engaged in this work
stays the first week with the pastor to help him
get started, and then moves on to the next
church. He has testified that it is the most
satisfying ministry he has had in his years of
missionary experience. The expressions of
appreciation from pastors and believers are
numerous. Certainly here is an area where
missionaries can develop a satisfying ministry
which will help the churches to become fruitful
in evangelism and church development.

Developing Church Schools

Probably the idea of Sunday schools as we
know them in the United States cannot be transferred without modification to the foreign field.
Nevertheless, the operation of a church school
with classes for different ages can be a very
fruitful endeavor. The primary objective, of
course, is the imparting of scriptural knowledge
to the converts. A secondary benefit is the
developing of teachers and workers as they

become active in the church and assume responsibility for classes. Some have found that the church school can also become an arm for evangelism by starting branch schools in new areas with the perspective that these might develop into new churches.

The area conferences in Latin America appointed Sunday school committees with the special obligation of fostering the advancement of this type of work. The Sunday school effort joins hands with Christian education in preparing materials for lay worker training and teacher training. This effort also gives a scope of ministry for both missionaries and nationals to the church as a whole and promises to be a fruitful aspect of missionary involvement.

LITERATURE

Even in the main languages outside of English, evangelical literature for evangelism, Christian maturity, and ministerial development is very inadequate. Some of this is being corrected in the principal languages such as Spanish, Portuguese, and French, but there is much to be done in this area.

Early in the history of the development of the work in Latin America, the need for literature was foreseen. The effort began with providing Sunday school quarterlies, but developed to include tracts, paper-covered books, textbooks, etc. Here again is a ministry which usually is beyond the reach of any single national church. In Latin America there are many Spanish-speaking countries, and so one publishing effort can serve them all without needlessly duplicating the effort in each country. This again provides a very much-needed

service to the churches, and both missionaries
and nationals can find a fruitful ministry in
this effort. Naturally, such a program would
have to be modified as one ministers in a
smaller language group. However, after the
Scriptures have been translated into the
language, missionaries can serve the national
church by further providing needed literature.

EVANGELISM

The area conferences also appointed committees on evangelism with the idea of stepping up
the evangelistic activities of the established
churches and initiating plans for carrying the
gospel to unreached areas. The committee
approved some general plans for Latin America,
but encouraged particularly the establishing of
evangelism committees within each country which
would carry out the special emphasis as might
fit the situation best. Missionaries, of course,
are involved in this effort in planning with
the national brethren the places for campaigns
and helping with the arrangements for workers,
literature, etc. Sometimes missionaries themselves have been the evangelists. The missionary's ministry in evangelism is dealt with in
some detail in the previous chapter, while a
general plan for total evangelism is elaborated
in Chapter 10, "Goals for Missions."

In this chapter we have endeavored to show
how missionaries may find new avenues of service
that will meet outstanding needs of the national
church even though they are no longer in a
pioneer church planting ministry. Such helps
are normally welcomed by national leaders.
Missionaries working in an area where a national
church has developed should consider the pressing needs that the church faces and endeavor to
find ways of meeting them.

9

The Missionary's
Spiritual Influence

The ministry of the missionary is essentially
spiritual. This is true whether he is engaged
in evangelistic work, administrative work,
office work, or teaching. The national church
stands in grest need of a spiritual ministry
which will inspire the Christians and give an
example to its leadership. It was pointed out
in a previous chapter that a national church
seldom closes its doors to a man that manifests
the fruit of the Spirit, and has an anointed
ministry in the Word, regardless of his nationality or race.

THE KEY TO SUCCESS

In all that we have discussed in the previous
chapters, whether it is the importance of a
missionary's relationship to his fellows or his
activities in missionary ministry, the key
to his success in the long run will be the
vitality and depth of his own spiritual life.
Jesus made this point clear to his disciples

before they were to begin their world ministry
when he compared himself to the True Vine and
the disciples to branches and told them that
they were ordained to bring forth fruit (John
15:16).

This fruit included both activity and character (Gal. 5:22-23), and the disciples were
instructed that in order to produce such fruit,
they must remain in union with the Vine. "Without me ye can do nothing" (John 15:5).

Missionary productivity and deep spirituality
go hand in hand. It was the renowned Hudson
Taylor who dedicated his life to China who wrote
the beautiful treatise on Union and Communion.
True faith will move mountains, but how important it is for us to remain in Christ so that
faith can operate through us.

Most of the problems which the missionary con-
fronts have their solution in his own spiritual
life and vitality. Many problems of relationships can be traced back directly to carnal
attitudes on the part of the participants..
Many obstacles before the church will yield to
intercessory prayer characterized by faith.
Today too little emphasis is placed on the
spiritual nature of missionary work. Missionaries find their slot in the work on the field
as a teacher, or as an administrator, and quite
often they feel that this is all that should be
expected of them. But there is so much more!
What about the consuming burden for those places
where the name of Christ is not yet named? Where
is the man who with Paul carries the problems of
"all the churches?" (2 Cor. 11:28, 29). Where
is the love that suffers with the weak and
offended? How can we expect the national
brethren to have a pastor's heart if we approach
our own task with an air of professionalism and
detachment?

THE MISSIONARY AS EXAMPLE

The missionary should be an example of Christian character. The fruit of the Spirit should mature in our lives. To our shame, we must confess that there is often a great gap between our preaching and our living. We preach about the wondrous love of God, and lose patience when our companions do not live up to our expectations. Quarrels develop in the missionary family that grieve the Spirit, and lower the spiritual tone of the church.

In some cultures, losing one's patience and speaking roughly to a friend or brother is almost an unpardonable sin. How we need to dwell in the Vine so that the fruit of righteousness and love is revealed in our lives! God grant that we too may be able to say, "Be ye followers of me even as I also am of Christ." Not all of us will be known as great men and not all of us will attain great ministries, but God grant that when we have finished our course on the field where God has placed us, Christian and unsaved alike will be able to say, "There was a man of God."

THE MISSIONARY AS SPIRITUAL LEADER

There is a constant need for spiritual emphasis in the work of God. There is a need for the prophetic voice that calls God's people to the fulfillment of His will. Times of spiritual refreshing--outpourings of the Spirit--are needed. It is a part of the spiritual ministry of the missionary to show the way. Praying Hyde proved that it could be done in India. Jonathan Goforth led the way in China. It is said that in the time of the Korean revival, when hindrances and barriers were presented that would seem to endanger the work, the church,

missionaries, and nationals alike would go to
their knees in prayer until the obstacle was
overcome and the Spirit of God could continue
His work. The presence of men in the church
that know how to pray and wage spiritual warfare
spells the difference between victory and defeat.

Leading the Church to Revival

The greatest contribution that the missionary
can make to the church in any country is a
spiritual contribution. His ability as an
administrator and organizer may be important but
it pales beside that of being a spiritual leader,
able to encourage the church, bringing it into
an atmosphere of revival through his teaching,
praying, and the spiritual impact of his life.

God gave to Solomon the key for revival for
the nation of Israel in times of national dis-
tress. "If I shut up heaven that there be no
rain, or if I command the locusts to devour the
land, or if I send pestilence among my people:
If my people, who are called by my name shall
humble themselves and pray, and seek my face,
and turn from their wicked ways; then will I
hear from heaven, and will forgive their sin,
and will heal their land" (2 Chron. 7:14).

Joel, chapter 2 contains the great promise of
the outpouring of the Spirit, especially in
verse 28. Earlier the prophet outlines the spiritual preparation needed to bring such blessings
about (Joel 2:12-19). These include repentance,
humbling of self, unity among God's people, and
intercession.

Charles G. Finney maintained that revival
follows spiritual laws like the laws of a tem-
poral harvest. He insisted that if we prepare
the soil of the heart, God would send the rain

and sunshine and give the increase that is
needed.

Missionaries should see themselves primarily
as channels of God's grace and blessing to the
needy people to whom they minister. Jesus
pointed out that even the need for workers for
the ripened harvest field is to be met by spiritual means. *"Pray ye* therefore the Lord of the
harvest that He would send forth laborers into
His harvest field" (Matt. 9:37). In the final
analysis the great task of world evangelism will
not be accomplished by programs, as needful as
these are, nor by human ingenuity alone "For it
is not by might nor by power, but by my spirit
saith the Lord" (Zech. 4:6).

10

Goals in Missions

As we acquire knowledge of the problems and
needs related to our task, we should endeavor
to apply it to our own situation. What is the
goal for the missionary's own life and field?
What should he expect to accomplish within the
next five-year period?

Probably much missionary effectiveness is
lost because the missionary has failed to outline for himself specific goals for his own
ministry. Too many times, the missionary does
that which is next at hand, that seems to
require his immediate attention, without planning for the accomplishment of the main objectives of his missionary effort. The missionary
is pushed by circumstances, and he ends his day,
his week, his year and his term without having
actually done the things that he intended to do.
Discipline of time is important. The missionary
must learn to distinguish between pressures from
circumstances and people, and his obligation to
fulfill his divine call. It will help to set

goals, and then plan the ways that those goals can become realities.

For any who might question the spiritual aspect of setting goals, it should be pointed out that Moses had a goal when he led the people out of Egypt. Jesus Christ Himself set a goal for the church when he gave the commission to preach the gospel to every creature. Paul in his writings set a goal for Christian maturity.

Applying this to our present and future situation, let us set goals for spiritual maturity, for our leadership, and for evangelism.

THE GOAL OF SPIRITUAL MATURITY

How do we expect our churches on the mission field to develop within the next few years? What should be our goal for the churches as to spirituality, biblical knowledge, worship, holiness, charity, and body ministry? How can the missionary help the church attain these goals?

MATURE LEADERSHIP

What kind of leadership does the church need? I am sure that we can agree that leadership should be progressive in the proper sense of the word. The Church needs leadership that will plan for the future and be able to adapt to the changes that come to every nation and church. Too many pastors and leaders feel they have done their part when they simply *maintain* the wheels of the work in motion, without having any definite concept of their goals. Leaders should be men of *vision* and *faith*.

Then the Church requires a leadership that is unselfish. A leader that is ambitious for personal position, gain, or comfort, and who

makes decisions on the basis of how these
matters affect him, cannot be a true leader of
the Church of Christ. A good leader, as a good
shepherd, must give his life for the sheep.

Leadership should be *knowledgeable*. It is
incumbent upon missionaries to find the way to
help leaders to develop their spiritual understanding. Leadership should not depend upon
borrowed knowledge. It must be personal and
experiential.

Then a leader must be *impartial*. He must
realize that he is to serve the entire church
and not just his friends. He must speak and act
the truth even when friends do not approve.

How we can help such leadership to develop
cannot be answered in a simple paragraph.
Actually, this is one of our life-time tasks.
Our example, our teaching, our trust in our
national leaders, all play their part. Finally,
of course, the national leader's own experience
will have to teach him. Above all, attitudes
are more important than gifts. God looks for
faithful men. The ability will come later (2
Tim. 2:2). The true leader must be God's man
and seek to please Christ above everything else.

GOAL OF TOTAL EVANGELISM*

The purpose of a plan of evangelism is to
enable us to obey the scriptural injunction to

*Some of the main steps in this plan for Total
Evangelism are taken from a paper *A Practical
Plan for Total Evangelism*, which grew out of a
meeting of national executives and missionaries
of the Assemblies of God in Central America in
Matagalpa, Nicaragua, and was assigned to missionary Ralph D. Williams for proper elaboration.

"look upon the fields," to find practical means for mobilizing the entire church in the effort of evangelism, and provide a vehicle through which the Holy Spirit can work in carrying out that which is His plan and purpose for the area.

In order to put into effect a comprehensive plan for total evangelism, there must be preparation and effort made on three levels: first, the missionaries, then the national leadership, and third, the pastors and their congregations. (We are addressing missionaries and place the responsibility first on them. Of course, it could be that a national leader would take the initiative in vision and inspiration.) To accomplish this it would be well to arrange for separate meetings with the groups mentioned in order to inspire their enthusiastic support, and work with them in the carrying out of the effort.

Motivation

Motivation is a key to success of any combined effort. There are two spiritual sources of motivation: the Word of God and the Holy Spirit. The first step when these groups come together is to inspire the group as to the scripturalness and practicality of a plan of total evangelization. There are many scriptures that show that Christ intends that the whole world shall hear the gospel. This includes "every creature."

The next step is to show the possibility of realizing the task. One person cannot do it alone. The solution is to *divide the task* into areas, zones, and individual churches, so that each entity, and finally each individual, can see where he fits into the program.

Once it is shown that it is God's will, and that it is something that can be accomplished through the power of the Holy Spirit, the next step is to initiate a plan of action.

The plan of action will begin by defining the area that is to be included in the effort (country, state, region).

The next step is to carry the plan of action to every level of the church, beginning with the national executives and then into the sectional areas and to the pastors.

Such a plan can logically be divided into two areas: the first area will be that which can be reached by the activity of the local churches. If a church is in a large city, the local church will find much room for activity in the city itself. Churches in smaller towns can decide which neighboring towns they will enter, or in which communities they will establish out-stations and branch churches.

The second area of concern will be the responsibility of the executives together with the missionaries. This has to do with the establishing of new churches in towns or cities where no church is established as a starter.

Providing for Total Evangelism

The planning must include, first of all, the workers. This may include the securing of evangelists, whether from outside the country or from the national churches and organization.

The second concern perhaps will be the providing of proper *tools for evangelism*. This will include literature to back up the evangelistic

outreach. Also included will be plans for the
use of radio and the setting up of campaigns in
strategic areas.

The *financial aspect* of the outreach will
have to be considered and a practical plan
evolved. Local churches should be included in
the financial plan of total evangelism.

It should be remembered that it is not
enough to outline a plan. For the plan to be
successful, there must be provision for following through. National executives and missionaries must take the project on their hearts and
give encouragement, advice and prayer support
to the effort. It may be advisable for the
national executives to designate a special
period of time for the churches to concentrate
on these efforts. For example, a certain goal
may be announced for a given year in which each
church should mother a new church. Some
national churches have designated a specific
year as "The Year of Total Evangelism" for
their country.

The Local Assembly

One of the most vital aspects of the plan of
total evangelism is the mobilization of the
local assembly to carry out the work of evangelizing their immediate community and surrounding
areas.

In order for the local church to carry on an
aggressive evangelism program, workers need to
be prepared in two areas: first, the local
worker who will preach in the outstations and
attempt to develop branch churches; then the
total membership which should be encouraged to
engage in personal evangelism and saturation
evangelism in a house-to-house ministry.

All levels of workers should be gathered for workers' weekly prayer meetings and study. This should be carried out on both the local and regional levels, although the regional level may have to limit such meetings to once a month. In this meeting reports will be presented and there should be an exchange of ideas and experiences as to methods employed. Naturally, this type of activity prepares the heart for periods of fervent prayer, which brings the blessings of God upon the church and the activities of the individual members.

PLANNING FOR REACHING GOALS

We are now thinking of individual missionary goals to be established in relation to a particular country.

The missionary should earnestly seek God to find out what his part will be in reaching the goal of total evangelism. This is more than an intellectual exercise. Should he change his location? Could God be calling him to devote more time to evangelism?

The missionary also can use his influence with the leadership of the national organization. The national executives need to see that it is their responsibility not only to take care of the churches that already exist, but to do some positive planning for the "regions beyond." Here is another area of contribution that the missionary can make to evangelism through instructing and stimulating the national church to become effective in its outreach.

It is important that the missionary not simply draw up plans himself and then expect the national brethren to come along. Rather he should share his burden with the brethren, but

in the actual working of the plans, he would do
well to let the ideas come from the national
brethren themselves with perhaps an occasional
suggestion and stimulation from his own thinking.
It is in this type of planning that the true
partnership with the national church evolves.

One question that he could well explore with
the national brethren is whether a mission could
be established. What about reaching an indigenous tribe? When will the national church
establish a missions department so that the
local churches become a part of the world-wide
outreach of the church?

Other questions to be considered are: what
has been done in the country under consideration
in the area of *evangelistic campaigns*? What
more can be done? Where are the strategic
cities in which campaigns should be held? Has
an adequate follow-up been implemented? Have
new churches been established as a result of
these efforts?

Today's world calls for decisive missionary
action. The opportunities to make a meaningful
contribution to world evangelism have never been
greater. In establishing goals for his personal
ministry, the missionary should not simply
depend upon human reasoning, or "pick his goals
out of the air," but rather see himself as a
channel for the fulfilling of the divine purpose
of God in world evangelism. This means that the
missionary must be a man led and inspired by the
Spirit of God. The Holy Spirit will lead him
in such a way that plans made will fit the culture and the people and will bring about hte
greatest success possible.

What a challenge faces the missionary today!
He lives in a strategic period in the history

of the world and of the Church. He is called of
God to carry out God's purposes in today's world.
He has a clear mandate from the scriptures and
divine guidance is open to him if he will but
bring his own life in tune with the divine
program.

We see great things ahead. With the national
church carrying the administration of the work,
the missionary can be freed from the obligations
of such details. He can devote more time for
prayer, Bible study, and evangelism. He can
return once again to the true missionary ministry which is a spiritual contribution which will
plant, establish, expand, and strengthen the
Church in the land of his calling.

Bibliography

ASSEMBLIES OF GOD, DIVISION OF FOREIGN MISSIONS
    1973 *The Missionary Manual of the Assemblies*
          of God, Springfield, Missouri.

GERBER, Vergil, ed.
    1971 *Missions in Creative Tension: The Green
          Lake '71 Compendium*, South Pasadena,
          California, William Carey Library.

HODGES, Melvin L.
    1973 *A Guide to Church Planting*, Chicago,
          Illinois, Moody Press.

    1971 *The Indigenous Church*, Springfield,
          Missouri, Gospel Publishing House.

McGAVRAN, Donald A., ed.
    1972 *Eye of the Storm: The Great Debate in
          Mission*, Waco, Texas, Word Books.
          [Enlarged edition published 1977 by Wil-
          liam Carey Library under the title, *The
          Conciliar-Evangelical Debate: The Cru-
          cial Documents, 1964-1976.*]

McGAVRAN, Donald A.
    1970 *Understanding Church Growth*, Grand
          Rapids, Michigan, Eerdmans.

MARQUEZ, Jairo
    1966 *Anatomia del Gringo*, Bogota, Colombia,
          Ediciones Tercer Mundo.

SCHERER, James A.
    1972 "Three Essentials in 'Salvation Today,'"
          Evangelical Missions Quarterly, Vol. 7,
          No. 4, Summer 1972.

WAGNER, C. Peter, ed.
    1972 *Church/Mission Tensions Today*, Chicago,
          Illinois, Moody Press.

WAGNER, C. Peter
    1970 *Latin American Theology*, Grand Rapids,
          Michigan, Eerdmans.

Melvin L. Hodges is an associate professor of missions at the Assemblies of God Graduate School in Springfield, Missouri, and is presently serving on an interim basis as dean of the Missions Division.

Dr. Hodges began his missionary career in 1936 with his appointment to El Salvador, Central America, and in 1954 began a twenty year period in the office of Field Secretary for Latin America and the West Indies. During his years as field secretary, he supervised the missionary effort in twenty-six countries. He encouraged the development of specialized ministries in evangelism, Sunday school, literature and Christian education.

Widely known in evangelical circles for his book, *The Indigenous Church*, which sets forth principles of church planting, Dr. Hodges has helped shape the missionary policy of the Assemblies of God and other evangelical missions.